HOPING AGAINST HOPE

A SELECTION

of modern-day healing miracles

compiled by
John Mikkelsen

Published by Stepping Stone Press
164 S. Highland Ave.
Pearl River, N.Y. 10965

Hoping Against Hope

A selection of modern-day healing miracles

compiled by John Mikkelsen

Published by
Stepping Stone Press
164 S. Highland Ave.
Pearl River, N.Y. 10965

First Edition
ISBN 0-9636935-0-6
$12.95 Softcover

This book is dedicated to all of the Christian ministries who, in the face of scorn, ridicule and rejection, have taught the word of God faithfully, accurately, consistently and with passion. To each of you: be encouraged. There is a remnant on the earth that hears and responds to the truth.

My son attend to my words: consent and submit to my sayings. Let them not depart from your sight; keep them in the center of your heart. They are life to those who find them, and healing and health to all their flesh.
Proverbs 4:20-22

A special expression of gratitude to Charles Woehrle from whom I first heard the truth.

"The Heavens And The Earth Shall Pass Away, But My Words Will Never Pass Away" Jesus – Matthew 24:35

TABLE OF CONTENTS

My prayer for you

Father, I ask You, in Jesus name, to bless each reader of this book. I ask that you use these testimonies to build their hope and strengthen their faith, so that they too can overcome all of the works of the enemy which come against them. Amen.

Hoping
Against Hope

*How to maintain your hope
— and build your faith —
when all human hope is gone.*

The Bible defines faith as the substance of things *hoped* for, the evidence of things not seen. That word *hoped* is the key to the equation. Faith is built upon hope. When the doctor says: "The cancer has gone too far, there is no hope," and you accept that prognosis, your basis for faith is destroyed.

This book contains fifteen testimonies of people who had very little hope of overcoming the physical assault on their bodies, yet each was healed when they learned to allow the word of God — the Bible — to build their faith to overcome human hope. They learned to pit Bible-based hope against human hope. *To hope against hope.*

The most dramatic illustration of this is the story of Abraham and Sarah. God told them they would have a baby, and that Abraham, who was at that time childless, would become the father of many nations. In other words they would have so many descendents they would populate entire nations.

There was a problem: Abraham was over a hundred years

old at the time and Sarah was about ninety. She was long past menopause. She had never been fertile; had never had children. But....God had spoken.

Picture that situation. Do you know a man a hundred years old with a wife ninety years old? There may be such a couple in a nursing home in your community. Can you imagine that man impregnating that woman and that woman giving birth to a healthy child? Of course that is medically impossible. Scientifically it could not happen. If you know something of human biology you know why it could not happen. There is no egg in the womb. There is no motility in the sperm. There is no way.

And, yet, Abraham chose to believe God rather than his own senses. Romans 4:18 says: *"...Abraham — human reason for hope being gone — hoped on in faith that he should become the father of many nations, as he had been promised."*

Of course we all know the story. Sarah became pregnant. Abraham did become the father of many nations. Many on the earth today are his descendants; children of that promise.

                    *   *   *

The purpose of this book is to raise your hopes; to encourage you to believe the promises of God which will heal you. If your god isn't a god of healing miracles, drop him, her, or it, and turn to the living God; the One who calls things that be not as though they were; the One who promises all things to those who have faith.

One of the biggest hindrances to our healing is the erroneous belief that God is the author of sickness and disability. The Bible does not teach that. It teaches that there is a renegade spirit loose in the world. He is called satan, and the Bible says that it is he who has come to kill to steal and destroy. It is satan who has laid the trap to steal your health, destroy your peace of mind and kill you.

God has already taken care of your healing. He has sent Jesus into the world, and He has sent ministries into the world to point you to Jesus, the healer. One of the titles given to Jesus is "The Great Physician."

Search these truths out for yourself in your own Bible. Be very selective about your sources of information. There are a number of loud voices in pulpits today who teach what the Bible calls: *"The traditions of men, which make the word of God of no effect."* Find a minister who knows the word of God, believes it, and practices it.

Be wary of denominationalism. It is divisive. It is confusing. God is not a Roman Catholic, or a Norwegian Lutheran, a Jehovah's Witness, a charismatic Pentecostal or whatever your pet denomination may be. God is God. He has spoken in His word, the Bible. Find out what He has said. Obey it, and prosper.

God is not your problem. The Bible says He has sent His word to heal you. He has said: *"My people perish because of a lack of knowledge."* You are sick essentially because you do not know that healing is available to you. You do not know who you are in Jesus Christ. Many people think God made them sick so that they can become better people through their suffering. The Bible doesn't teach that, and as long as you believe that you will have a very difficult time trying to use your faith to receive your healing.

At one point the religious leaders of Jesus' day were teaching that Jesus cast out demonic spirits by using demonic spirits. Jesus called them to Himself and taught them. You can read it in the third chapter of the book of Mark in the Bible. He said to them: *"How can satan cast out satan? If a kingdom is divided against itself, that kingdom cannot stand. And if a house is divided against itself, that house cannot stand."*

Don't you be a house divided against yourself. Don't be double minded. The Bible says the double minded can expect nothing from God. As long as you think God made you sick, you cannot even go to the doctor in faith to try get healed. You must get your thoughts focused to attain your healing. God gets no glory from your sickness. He does get glory from your healing. You get your healing by using your faith.

The Bible tells us that without faith it is impossible to please God. Faith comes by hearing, and hearing by the word of God. The word of God is the Bible. Read it. Believe it. Act on it. You inherit all of the promises of God by patiently using your faith.

The people you will read about in this book are no different from you. Each of them overcame the circumstances of their lives and attained victory over serious afflictions. You can do the same.

*   *   *

Note: The names of some of the people in this book have been changed for reasons personal to them. They are all real, and the words are their own.

"If I regard iniquity in my heart the Lord will not hear. But certainly God has heard me; He has attended to the voice of my prayer. Blessed be God, who has not turned away my prayer, nor His mercy from me." Psalm 66:18-19

*   *   *

"Be anxious for nothing, but in everything by prayer and supplication, with thanksgiving, let your requests be made known to God; and the peace of God, which surpasses all understanding, will guard your hearts and minds through Christ Jesus." Philippians 4:6-7

Shawn Jasna

" We do not wrestle against flesh and
blood, but against principalities,
against powers, against the rulers of
the darkness of this age, against
spiritual wickedness in high places."
Ephesians 6:12

March 23, 1985 Shawn Jasna, 15, was visiting in his old
neighborhood in Sallisaw, Oklahoma. He was at the home of
a friend with whom he had grown up but hadn't seen since
the Jasna's moved to Broken Arrow, Ok. a year before. His
friend had discovered hard rock music, and he invited Shawn
back to his bedroom to hear a new record by a hard rock
group. From the speakers blared a song titled "Billy's Got A
Gun."

Without warning a shot blasted out, the report drowning
out the noise from the speakers. Shawn dropped to his
knees, a .38 caliber bullet buried deep in his brain.

"I remember something hitting my head and knocking me
to the ground. I got up and ran into the wall. Then some
people were carrying me down the hall and turning my head
to the side so I wouldn't choke on the blood. That's all I
remember about the shooting," Shawn said.

Twenty miles away, just across the Oklahoma-Arkansas border, Shawn's parents, The Rev. Rick and Linda Jasna, were visiting Linda's mother in the intensive care unit of Sparks Regional Medical Center in Fort Smith where she was being treated for a cerebral hemorrhage.

Rick Jasna

I took the phone call at the nurse's station in the intensive care unit. It was an ambulance attendant. He said they were going to transport my son to Sparks Hospital where we were because they couldn't treat his injury in Sallisaw. All he told me was that Shawn had a gunshot wound to the head, and that it did not look good.

About three seconds after I hung up the phone God spoke to me and said: "This is my battle; are you going to give it to me?" It was just that clear. I had been intensively studying the Bible for some time. We knew who we were in Christ Jesus according to the Bible. We knew God's promises to us. We knew we could not get into agreement with what had just taken place. We had a right to choose. We knew that satan is the one who has come to kill. We knew he did not have a right to do what he had just done because we serve God.

The Lord told me next to go and pray and to begin to claim some things. I was shaking when we went into a small room there in the hospital to pray. The first thing God told me in prayer was: "I want you to separate yourself from every earthly way." He also said: "I will tell you what to say and I will tell you what not to say." Then He told me to cast out the spirit of death. As soon as we did that a peace came over Linda and me. I could feel fear as close as my nose trying to close in on us, but it wasn't on me and it wasn't on my wife.

It was all around us though. While my wife took care of the hospital paper work I went down to the emergency dock where they would be bringing him in. I stood there and prayed in tongues and waited.

Linda Jasna

While we were in that little room praying we asked that every hand that touched Shawn, directly or indirectly, in that hospital be anointed by God. All of my relatives were there in the hospital because of my mother's surgery the day before. Some of them were believers and some were non-believers. We had that to deal with. The first thing I did when we left that little prayer room was to call the prayer intercessors.

Rick Jasna

The Lord was constantly giving me direction in what to do as I prayed in tongues and waited for the ambulance. He told me to send forth ministering angels and to not listen to any unbelief. I knew that meant people that we loved who would want to see Shawn but who were unbelievers. I had just seen in Linda's Mother's case where they would gather around and talk about how bad she looked and how she was probably going to die.

When the ambulance finally arrived a new wave of fear swept in. It was like an ocean trying to knock me off my feet. In the spirit I saw devastation everywhere. It was all around, trying to get in, but it wasn't in me. Just moments before the ambulance pulled up God spoke to me again and told me to go and talk to the head nurse who was standing nearby. I had no idea what to say to her. I just went over to her and opened my mouth and said: "I choose, because of who I am in Jesus Christ, and because of what my Father has shown me, that I will not leave my son. I will be with him at all times." She said: "Ok, ok." God had prepared her heart.

They brought him out of the ambulance fast and wheeled him straight into the emergency room. I had to run to keep up, but I was right there with him. Blood was coming out of both ears, out of his nose and mouth. His shirt, pants and even socks were soaked in blood. He was as white as a piece of paper. I could see brain tissue coming out of the entry wound just above his right ear. He wasn't breathing on his own. One of the attendants was squeezing this bag to make him breath. When she quit squeezing Shawn just lay there, his chest not moving.

The Lord told me to lay hands on him and pray. I put my hands on his chest, and my wife put her hands on his head. The woman who was squeezing the breathing bag stopped and looked at me eyeball to eyeball. She didn't say anything, but her expression said: "Don't you realize he is dead. There is nothing you can do. This is kind of dumb." She had been squeezing that bag for thirty minutes, and Shawn wasn't breathing.

I didn't pray loudly or boldly. My voice was shaky. I said: "Father, in the name of Jesus we claim total healing for our son. We will not accept anything less; not because of who we are, but because of what Your word says, and we are standing on Your word." Then I talked to satan. I took authority over him in the name of Jesus, and I called his assignment against my son to be null and void.

As soon as I prayed I had the peace of God on the inside of me. I knew this was a tragic thing. Spiritually, it was completely out of order. I knew that satan had no right to do this. When I finished the prayer and turned away from my son I started laughing on the inside of me. That was the joy of the Lord rising up in me. I had accomplished what He wanted done in that prayer. At that moment satan spoke to me and said: "I've killed your so-called preacher son. I've put a bullet in his brain, and he is not going to preach God's word anymore."

That really set me laughing because the Bible says that satan is a liar. The truth isn't in him. Satan sent several people our way to try to get us off our stand on the word of God. We were past being influenced by man. We were in the battle, and the battle was the Lord's. We had to stand.

The neurosurgeon, who was the same man who had operated on my mother-in-law the previous day, after examining Shawn, said: "He is too far gone. There is just not much we can do for him. It is in the hands of God." Well, I was in agreement with that last part. Shawn was in God's hands.

The doctor said that he would clean and irrigate the wound, but that he couldn't possibly get out all of the metal particles, hair, bone and blood clots that were in that wound. It was long and deep, and it went through both hemispheres of the brain. He told us that he would do his best, but he couldn't remove everything that should come out, including the bullet, without doing more damage to the brain.

The path of the bullet through the brain was as wide as my little finger. I saw the CAT scan, and on either side of the bullet's path you could see a wide area where the brain had been damaged by the concussion. There were metal particles all along the path.

When Shawn was in the operating room, and we were in the waiting room praying, I looked over at Linda, and I saw she was about to break. One of the things the Lord told me to do was not to get into any earthly way. This was a battle

situation, and we had to keep ourselves separated from man
and his ideas. I wouldn't let myself visit with people. I had to
separate myself and listen moment by moment to the Lord
and do what He was telling me to do.

When Linda started crying the Lord told me to go and talk to
her. I had no idea what to say to her. What can you say in a
situation like that when her son has got a bullet in his brain
and the doctors are telling you he cannot live. I opened my
mouth, and I said: "If you are going to cry you are going to
have to do it in the spirit. If you can't do that you are going
to have to get away and leave me alone. There are things that
have to be done now in the spirit." There was no way on
earth I wanted to say that to her, but I knew it was the Lord,
and I said it.

Linda Jasna

   If Rick had come over and tried to console me, and put his
arm around me, and turned his attention to comforting me, I
would have known by that that he didn't really believe
Shawn was healed. If Rick had given me just a little bit of
sympathy I would have lost it. There would have been no
getting me back.

Rick Jasna

   While Shawn was in the operating room all of the relatives
came to the hospital. The boy who shot Shawn came in. He
was almost like a son to me. The boys had played together
since they were five years old. I knew enough about the
word of God, and about the will of God, and about satan's
devices, to know this boy had been used by satan. It wasn't
really the boy who had shot my son. It was satan. I knew
that. I had already forgiven the boy in my heart, but now

God spoke to me and He told me to go tell the boy he was forgiven.

I looked across the room and there were about thirty people there, and they were just devastated. The boy was sitting across the room, and he was hurting. He was just rocking back and forth. I'd seen combat troops in Vietnam doing that. He'd been crying. It was at that point that I absolutely knew that my son was healed.

I realized at that moment that I had no feelings as to whether my son was going to make it or not. My emotions were no longer involved. But, I did have some feelings toward that boy who had shot my son. I had compassion for him. He had been used by satan. There was a spirit of suicide on him. When I realized that, I knew my son was healed, and my concern was no longer for Shawn.

I told Linda to get hold of the prayer intercessors and get that spirit of suicide cast off the boy. I walked over to him, and I called him by name and said: "I forgive you, and I do not hold anything against you." That was the only time I cried. I put my arm around him and I hugged him. He received my forgiveness, and it was like he didn't understand any more about what happened than anyone else. He was in shock. He had been used.

Then I had to go off by myself, away from everyone. There must have been fifty people there by then. Classmates from Shawn's school were arriving, family friends, and prayer intercessors. When people would come up to me in the hallway and try to talk to me I would just turn away. It was hard to do, but God told me to do that. Shawn was in surgery for four hours.

One of the medical staff told us: "Just so you can prepare yourself I'll tell you what is going to happen to your son.

Because of the extent of the injury his whole face is going to turn black. His eyes are going to swell right out of their sockets. There is going to be tremendous pressure on his brain, and that pressure is going to force his eyes out. Also, he will develop an extremely high fever." This was the head surgical nurse. He was a medical authority in that position. Logic would tell you that based on his training and experience you should just accept what he says.

But, through our knowledge of the word of God, I applied His word to that situation. I pointed my finger at the nurse and I said: "In the name of Jesus Christ of Nazareth my son will not turn black. He will not have swelling of the brain, and he will not have a high temperature." What I said was foolishness to the natural mind. The Bible says that the Holy Spirit will rise up in you and give you the right things to say, and that was one of those times. But, I had the choice to either speak it out or to remain silent.

Linda Jasna

We had agreed in prayer for a total healing for Shawn. That was our decision. We weren't going to accept him just being alive, brain damaged, with no more life in him than a vegetable. We agreed in prayer for a total healing. Some people would have shut their faith down and quit with the person just being alive. They would have been grateful for that much. We don't have to settle for just being alive. We have been promised abundant life.

Rick Jasna

On the fifth day after Shawn was shot they took him out of the ICU and put him in a regular room. He was sitting up in bed. He looked normal. He had a bandage on his head, and he was very weak. I was sitting in a chair watching him, and I noticed that when he looked at me one of his eyes didn't track with the other. He had had good vision while he was in the ICU. Now satan was trying to steal his vision. At that point, again, many people would have said: "Well, at least my son is back, even through his eyes are messed up. It's better than having a funeral. At least he's alive."

We had asked God just one time for Shawn's healing, and the rest of the time we were thanking Him for the healing. So, when I noticed Shawn was having vision problems I laid hands on him and I spoke to God and thanked Him again for Shawn's *total* healing, and I thanked Him for the knowledge that satan had no right to afflict him. I also spoke to Shawn's eyes (Jesus said to speak *to* the mountain) and I told them to work right, and to line up with the word of God.

Fifteen minutes later Shawn's main doctor came in and checked his eyes. An hour later an eye doctor came and gave Shawn a thorough eye examination. Between 3 p.m. and 11 p.m. five different medical authorities came and examined Shawn's eyes. Five people with medical authority agreed there was something wrong with Shawn's vision. My wife and I stood in agreement with the Word of God on the other side. We did not accept the medical diagnosis. The next morning Shawn's eyes were working perfectly.

When Shawn was in the ICU at time he looked at me as if he were in pain, and I would talk to him and tell him: "Shawn, you are going to have to stand on the word of God. You have got what it takes and you can do it. You are going to make it." He would nod his head in agreement. They only gave him four pain shots during the whole ordeal, and they weren't anything major. This was another thing that amazed the staff.

In the course of Shawn's hospitalization, as I separated myself from every worldly thing, and as I prayed in the spirit and with my understanding, my faith got so strong that I could not understand why the doctors could not understand that Shawn was healed. I got to the place where I really didn't care what the situation looked like. I was walking in the spirit. My son was healed. Everything got turned around. The natural world counted for nothing. The word of God was the only reality I knew.

Linda Jasna

Our whole family got into that strong position of faith because we had prayed together, we had studied the Bible together, and we had attended many faith building seminars and conventions as a family.

Our son Chad told me after the shooting: "Mom, I almost cried, but then I thought, if God is real, and He is, and if His word is true, and it is, then Shawn is healed, and he will be coming home in a few days, and there is no need to be upset."

The adults, including the kids Sunday school teachers, were amazed at the children's faith throughout this experience. They all stood firm.

Rick Jasna

As a family we had made ourselves available to hear the word of God. If there was some faith-building teaching going on within a two or three hour drive of our home we went. We bought good Bible teaching on cassette tape, and throughout our house that was what you would hear, from the children's bedrooms, the kitchen, everywhere. We fed on the word of God.

When satan tried to present that tragedy to us we were operating in the word of God as a family. We were all in agreement. What I saw in that emergency room was a tragedy. Spiritually it was completely out of order, and my family was not involved with it at the natural level. In the natural realm we should have been more upset than anyone, but through our knowledge of the Bible the power of the Holy Spirit was on my family, and that is what brought us through in victory.

Satan was mad because we were operating in the word of God, and he was not able to carry through on his plan to destroy my son. When Shawn was in the ICU a fire broke out there. Immediately I asked the Lord if I was to take him out of there. God said to me: "No, he is on holy ground. He is just fine. Leave him here."

Then on the seventh day of his hospitalization, when he was in a regular room, another fire broke out in the hospital. I was sitting in his room and I smelled the smoke. I opened the door to the hallway and it was solid smoke. I couldn't even see across the hall. Firemen were running up and down. A nurse came up with a wet towel over her face and told me to get back in the room and put a towel under the door. I didn't realize until later that the smoke didn't even affect me. It didn't bother my eyes or my breathing. I wasn't aware of it, except that I could see it. I had been praying in tongues for seven days.

Again I asked God if I should get Shawn out of there, and again He told me that he was on holy ground and was safe. He also told me to take authority over the situation, and I did. In moments the fire was out, and the firemen set up big fans to blow the smoke out of the halls. How often do you hear about a fire in a hospital? How often do you hear about two fires in a hospital in one week? It was satan.

Linda Jasna

When Shawn was in surgery I asked Rick how long we were going to be there. He told me that we would leave the hospital with Shawn in ten days. I was having to deal with all of the relatives, police, hospital administration, friends, and my mind was telling me that ten days for something as serious as this wasn't possible.

I was hearing all the voices of the world, and that was why I was questioning. Rick was thinking at first that he was going to take Shawn home as soon as they got the bleeding stopped and put a bandage on him. Whenever the relatives or anyone would try to talk to Rick I would deal with them. He wouldn't talk to them. He didn't want to hear their unbelief. He just stayed before God.

Rick Jasna

The Lord told me that if I would stay in His word, and stand fast on what He gave me, I would understand the scriptures. The word of God, the Bible, has been given to us to deal with the issues of life. One of the things that greatly influences people — and we shouldn't allow it — is the attitudes of other people. People's attitudes have absolutely nothing to do with the word of God. The word of God is exact knowledge.

So when I laid my hands on my son to pray for him it was no small thing because that was what God had told me to do. In the natural realm laying hands on my son just didn't fit. It was like throwing out a grain of mustard seed. It seemed to be so small and worthless in the face of such a massive need. But, because it was the word of God it was bigger in my spirit than any of the circumstances.

I asked the doctor on the first day how long Shawn would have to be there because I knew he was hurting, and I wanted to get him out of there and take him home. The doctors told me only that I had to allow time for him to heal. God told me that Shawn would go home in ten days. On the ninth day I told the doctor: "Well, we get to take him home tomorrow don't we?"

The doctor said no. He said Shawn would have to stay for another four or five days. That news hit me like someone slapping my face. I couldn't understand that. I blurted out: "That's not what God said." The doctor told me they had given Shawn some medication and they needed to monitor him over the next four to five days. Then for a moment I thought, well, maybe I didn't hear from God, but immediately I got a check in my spirit, and I said, yes, I did to hear from God. I know His voice. I know what my Father said. So I knew that some way Shawn was going home the next day. I didn't know how.

About six o'clock that afternoon the doctor came to check Shawn again. I had already asked him about taking Shawn home the following day. He is a professional man. He knew his business, and I respected that. I had no right to badger him about this, so I didn't ask again. When he finished the examination he turned to me and told me that Shawn could go home the next day; ten days after he had been admitted. The doctor told me they would make arrangements for him to take the medication at home.

Linda Jasna

When Shawn was brought into the hospital we were told he could not live. After they cleaned out the wound in surgery and put him in the ICU they told us he still could not live. Then they said he might live for a time but he would stay in a coma, that he had massive brain damage. They said he would be a vegetable, and that he would never leave the hospital. They said he would have to stay in ICU for at least six months, if we were lucky and he lived that long. Shawn walked out of that hospital on his own two feet in ten days.

We had asked in prayer that Shawn not only be restored to good health, but that he be made better than he was before he was shot. The year before he had taken a physical exam through the high school so he could be on the athletic team. They discovered a 30 percent hearing loss in his right ear. After he was discharged from the hospital the same doctor tested his hearing again and it was perfect in both ears.

There was a jockey in the next cubicle to Shawn's in the hospital. He had a broken back and was told he would never walk again. When he saw Shawn healed he came to believe that supernatural healing is possible. We ministered to him, and he walked out of the hospital too.

Shawn finished 9th grade in home school after getting out of the hospital. The doctors ordered us to keep him quiet and not let him engage in sports. He still has that bullet in his brain. We really are a unique people because we stand on the word of God. We don't walk by sight, and the world cannot understand that.

Rick Jasna

Every step of the way I saw very clearly that the choices presented to us were strictly ours to make. We could freely choose what God had said, or we could choose what man was saying. The choice was always ours. Never did God just overwhelm us with His sovereign will. We could have received Shawn dead. That was what the world tried to give us. We could have received him alive but severely brain damaged. We could have received him crippled. But God told me right from the start: "This is My battle; are you going to give it to Me?"

What He was saying was, are you going to agree with My will and My word in all that comes against you in this matter, or are you going to agree with the world's assessment of the situation? You choose. In all of this we were operating in revelation knowledge; information coming directly from the spirit of God into our spirits. We didn't just quote selected Bible verses; but we did quote a great deal of scripture.

One of the great lessons we have learned is how to apply the word of God directly to the issues of life. We were praying in tongues, which the Bible says edifies us, and we were listening as God spoke to us. He did speak, and we did what He told us to do, moment by moment.

*   *   *

*"No weapon formed against you shall
prosper, and every tongue which rises
against you in judgement you shall
condemn. This is the heritage of the
servants of the Lord, and their
righteousness is from Me, says the Lord."*
Isaiah 54:17

"*...you do not have because you
do not ask.
You ask and do not receive
because you ask amiss...*"
James 4:2-3

*   *   *

"*He sent His word and healed them
and delivered them from their destructions.*"
Psalm 107:20

*   *   *

"*As for God, His way is perfect.
The word of the Lord is proven.*"
Psalm 18:30

Fred Gorini

*"For the word of God is living and
powerful, and sharper than any
two edged sword..." Hebrews 4:12*

In July of 1982, after suffering from back pain for a number of years, I went to a doctor and was told I had an advanced case of vertebral osteomyolitis. At the time I was a field engineer at Epcot Center in Florida. I was a project manager in charge of structural steel for a number of the buildings.

Through x-rays and CAT scans it was determined that one vertebral disk and vertebra had already disintegrated. I went to another doctor to get a second opinion, and his report was also very grave: an advanced case of bone disease. I was told to prepare myself for life in a wheelchair. They said there was also a very strong chance I would be paralyzed for the rest of my life. My spine was collapsing. You could see that on the x-rays. It was said to be irreversible.

Surgery was recommended. It was to be accomplished in two stages; first from the front, and then from the back. They planned to reinforce my spine with steel pins and plates. I was also told the chance of my getting through this surgery without suffering paralysis was very slim.

At that time, in prayer, the Spirit of the Lord said to me to decline the surgery. I was a Christian and I was involved in a lay ministry. I went on disability leave from my job for a period of six months. I was almost totally crippled. I was fitted with a brace, which was like an artificial spine, so that I could stand to my feet. During that six months I lay on a cot in my living room. I couldn't move. Sneezing, or having a bowel movement, would send me into spasms that would put me on the floor in a ball of pain. I could hardly stand or walk, even with the brace.

At this time we acquired cable t v, and I began watching the Christian programming on the PTL Satellite Network. One teacher in particular caught my attention: Kenneth Copeland. My first response to him was negative. I was a Pentecostal, and I thought to myself: "Who does this guy think he is?" But he had the precise message I needed in the situation I was in. I ordered some of his teaching tapes including a series called The Sower Soweth The Word. Those messages turned my life around.

Kenneth taught on *imaging* the word; about finding the word of God for your situation and then visualizing it. I searched the scriptures for verses about bones, and I found a number of them. One was Ezekiel 37:3-6 — *"And He said unto me, Son of man, can these bones live? And I answered, O Lord God, thou knowest. Again He said unto me, Prophecy upon these bones, and say unto them, O ye dry bones, hear the Word of the Lord. Thus saith the Lord God unto these bones; behold I will cause breath to enter into you, and ye shall live: and I will lay sinews upon you, and will bring flesh upon you, and cover you with skin, and put breath in you, and ye shall live; and ye shall know that I am the Lord."*

My bones were dying. They were being absorbed into my

body, I was told. I began to do what Kenneth Copeland said: *image the word.* I obtained some medical drawings which showed what a normal, perfect spine looked like. I prayed the word of God over my spine. I prayed with my understanding, and I prayed in the spirit. I visualized my spine being healed according to God's promises in the Bible.

In the six months I lay on that cot I took no medication, and I had no surgery. I went periodically to the doctors for progress reports. They kept telling me they couldn't help me unless I submitted to the surgery. My wife, who was in total agreement with me, continued to stand with me and speak only the word of God over my condition. We didn't dwell on the symptoms, and we didn't talk about the medical prognosis. We spoke of healing according to the Bible.

Many of our family members, even those who were considered to be people of faith, thought we were in error. I was 37 years old, and I had children and responsibilities, so naturally these family members thought I was throwing my life away by not having the operation. They were convinced I would be in a wheelchair if I didn't get some medical help soon.

My wife and I decided at that time to cut ourselves off from all negative thinking and speaking people. Even though they were well intentioned, they were destroying the faith we were trying to build up, so there were a number of people we avoided during this period.

During this time I was teaching a Bible study from the cot in the living room. I could hardly move. We laid hands on the sick and prayed for their recovery, even though I was the sickest person there. After six months like that I began to get back some mobility. I didn't have an instant healing. It was progressive. It took a while before I was completely healed.

In another six months I returned to work, and within a year I was led by the Lord, as a result of the whole experience, to start a church. It began in our home at the time I was on the cot teaching a Bible study. About two years after I was healed, and in the stress of the ministry, satan attack me again with the same symptoms of spinal disease and intense pain. Kenneth Copeland was holding a meeting in Orlando, and I was seated in the second row. My back was hurting then, and Kenneth looked straight at me. What he said to me was unrelated to anything he was teaching on at the moment. He said: "Strong, healthy bones."

That totally settled it for me. Satan was trying to make me sick again, but when the word of the Lord came through Brother Copeland in that way I got complete victory, complete healing, and I am still walking in divine healing.

During the six months I was on that cot the doctor's reports got progressively worse. I had to go in every month for an exam because of the workman's disability claim. After that six months in bed I heard the Spirit of God tell me to go back to work, and I did. I wore the brace for a few months. I stayed away from doctors for a while. After I went full time into the ministry I was in a hospital visiting some people on a ministerial visit when I met one of the doctors who had previously examined me. He asked me how in the world I was able to walk around. I told him my story, and he just shook his head and said: "Well, I guess there are miracles today."

I later met another of the doctors who had examined me. He was astounded, but not willing to credit the healing to God. People ask me if I have ever been back to have my spine x-rayed to confirm the healing and to actually see if that disintegrated disc and vertebra were restored. I thought about doing that, but I asked God in prayer if I should, and He asked: "Do you need that, son?" I told Him that I didn't require any medical proof. I have full mobility. I have no pain. I work out on a Nautilus exercise system. I can lift heavy things with no problem.

As I prayed about it the Holy Spirit told me: "If you were to have x-rays taken and they showed that you have no bones, I would still uphold you with the right hand of my power." So my faith is in God's word, and not in x-rays and medical reports. Satan wants us to reject God's word. If he can get us to reject the word, or to minimize it, then he can destroy our faith.

While I was on that cot, doubled up in pain, ministering healing to others, it was a constant battle to beat down the accusations of satan. Many who meant well kept telling me how foolish I was. People said, how can you be teaching healing when you are in severe pain and can hardly move?

That was a perplexing question, but it was through faith in the word of God. It was because I was keeping the word of God before my eyes. I was casting down vain imaginations that tried to exalt themselves above the word of God. I settled some things during that time. The book Bodily Healing In The Atonement by Dr. Roy Hicks and Kenneth Hagin helped a great deal as I studied it and made decisions. I became determined.

When I first came to the Lord I had been a drug user for 13 years. I was saved through studying and believing the Bible; the word of God. I wasn't in a church. I just read the Bible. No one was teaching me but the Holy Spirit. He said He will lead us into all truth. I was saved and delivered from drugs at that time. I made a decision based upon what I read in the word that healing was a part of my redemption and salvation. When things came up to cast doubt I would not allow myself to cross over that line into unbelief.

My wife stood with me as a solid covenant partner during those times. She was especially strong when I was on that cot and laying hands on people and praying for their healing. She was a source of great strength to me as she stood with me.

It was quite a trial. Many of the things I've written here about that experience I did not have understanding of while they were happening. I did have the Bible, even though I didn't fully understand what was going on. It was my acting on the truths I found in the Bible that brought the results. The word of God is true.

*   *   *

*"If any of you lacks wisdom, let him ask
of God, who gives to all liberally and
without reproach, and it will be given him.
But let him ask in faith, with no doubting,
for he who doubts is like a wave of the sea
driven and tossed by the wind."*

James 1:4-6

Tim Shaffer

*"And we desire that each one of you show
the same diligence to the full asurance of
hope until the end, that you do not become
sluggish, but imitate those who through
faith and patience inherit the promises."*
Hebrews 6:11-12

When I was in the fifth grade I got rheumatic fever. The
initial symptoms didn't last long, but the long term effect of
that disease is to destroy the heart muscle. Bacteria lodge in
the heart and slowly weaken the valves. After other
symptoms have passed, the action of the heart pumping
blood further erodes the valves. There was no outward sign
of the damage being done to my heart for ten years, but
eventually the damage showed up. I had known there was
something wrong with me, but I didn't know what. The first
symptom I noticed was my breathing. Exertion would leave
me breathless. The problem was diagnosed when I tried to
enlists in the Air Force in 1965.

Cardiologists told me I would live a basically normal life
with some restrictions. I would need regular exams, must

take antibiotics daily, and must not over exert myself. But, even with that, in 15 or 20 years, I would need heart valve surgery. The damaged valves would have to be replaced by plastic valves. They called the condition aortic and mitral valve insufficiency.

At the time they told me I would be needing heart valve surgery three out of four patients did not survive the operation. Presently the mortality rate is about one percent. However, once the valves are replaced with the plastic valves the surgery has to be repeated every ten years and a person can only have the operation about three times before the condition becomes inoperable. Moreover, I would have to take anti-clotting medicine for the rest of my life once I had the plastic valves installed.

I quickly got to know my physical limitations, and I used the illness to baby myself. I chose jobs that weren't physically demanding, excused myself from hard work, and manipulated my family and friends into letting me have first place in lines, the best seats, etc., because of my heart condition. But, what started as an excuse eventually became reality. There was little I could do without becoming tired.

It was February 1982 that my doctor told me it was time to have the corrective valve surgery. I had been going to doctors since I was 19 to have the condition monitored so they knew my full medical history. They had a thick file of electrocardiograms on me. I asked the doctor what would happen to me if I chose to not have the surgery. He told me that my health would continue to deteriorate, and that I would soon be walking only with great difficulty. Next I would be confined to a wheelchair, then bedridden, and, within five years at the most I would be dead.

That prognosis seemed plausible because I was

deteriorating, and I knew it. I was breathless much of the time. I could take very little exertion. I was having difficulty sleeping. I could only sleep propped up in a sitting position. If I tried to sleep laying down I couldn't breathe. Also, I was having chronic headaches, and I was tired all of the time. No matter how much I slept I couldn't get any energy. My fingers and toes were blue due to oxygen starvation because of poor blood circulation. One of the most disturbing symptoms was the feeling there was a constant weight on my chest. It wasn't pain, but a feeling as if someone were sitting on my chest; a constant heavy pressure.

When I heard that five-year death sentence from the doctors I went to the Lord in prayer. I said: "I've believed all my life that You are a God that heals, and I believe that You can heal me."I told Him that I would rather die than go through the valve surgery. I reasoned that if I were healed through surgery I would never know whether it was God or the doctors who healed me.

Shortly after that I attended a local church holding a healing service. I was sitting on the end of the row. The evangelist came down the row touching the heads of everyone on the end seats. When he got to me, he skipped me, and then continued on touching the others. I got really upset with God when that happened. I told Him: "God, I have waited years to be healed. This is a very desperate time for me. This is my last chance. Why?"

Then I heard His voice clearly in my spirit. He said: "I have control over every beat of your heart, and I decide when it will stop. Not you. Not the medical profession. Not a healer. I decide." With that I said: "Alright. I will go to three more healing services, and if there is no improvement in my condition I will submit to the surgery."

Just a few weeks later I was listening to a Christian tv program and heard Kenneth Copeland teaching on faith and patience. I order the cassette tapes, and then continued watching the program every week. I listened to those tapes over and over again. I would play them while I was getting ready to go to work, and I would play them when I got home. I bought a portable tape player and listened to them going to and from work and during my lunch hour. I listened to those tapes from two to four hours every day.

The more I listened the more my faith grew, and the more my faith was established, the more spiritually hungry I became. I worked at it. The one point I would stress to anyone believing God for physical healing is: STICK WITH IT. Give it the same kind of attention and dedication you would give to earning a college degree. You cannot be casual about it, and then say: "Well, I tried that faith stuff." This is the primary lesson I learned, and this lesson has carried over to every area of my spiritual life.

I became committed. I decided I was going to make a Bible study of healing my first priority, and that I would listen to teaching tapes until I had full manifestation of my healing. I spent many, many hours listening to tapes and studying the Bible in order to build my faith. I sought the Holy Spirit to give me the will to do it. When you have years of fear behind you, as I had, it takes many hours of listening to the word of God to overcome.

Kenneth Copeland's teaching series on fear was a great help to me. I listened to those tapes over and over again because I realized that fear was a major killer of faith. During that time I stopped eating lunch with my friends so that I could be by myself and concentrate on hearing those taped teachings. I stopped socializing. I almost became anti-social so that I would have the time to build my faith by hearing the word of God and absorbing spiritual sustenance.

I told myself over and over again that this was a life-or-death issue, and that I could not afford to play games or be casual about this. I had been playing games about standing on the word of God for twenty years, and the doctors were telling me I was dying. I had no more time to play religious games. Hearing the word of God became my first priority. I was renewing my mind.

It was interesting to me that the first set of teaching tapes I listened to was on faith and patience. Hebrews 6:12 says: *"... do not become sluggish, but imitate those who through faith and patience inherit the promises."* That's what I was going to do; imitate those who had set the example by attaining the promises.

It would have seemed logical to concentrate on what the Bible had to say about healing and make the study of physical healing my aim. I believe the Holy Spirit directed my study, and He knew I had to develop my faith in more areas of my life than just physical healing. The principle thing I needed to know at the outset was that I had to stick with it, and that is what I studied.

I came to know that if I persevered I would harvest not only a healing for my heart, but I would harvest in other areas of my life as well. I didn't actually begin to study the scriptural subject of healing until a year after I was healed.

After about three months of listening to teaching tapes and feeding my spirit on the word of God I realized one day that I had more energy. I hadn't been paying much attention to my body. My attention was on the word of God, and I was standing on that word. Some of my friends, people who knew me really well, began to comment about my skin color.

It was getting pink, and it hadn't been pink since they had known me. I had had a generally sallow look, and my fingers had been blue.

Other symptoms began to disappear, and I knew I had been healed. After two years I thought I really should go to the doctors and get an examination for the sake of my mother. It can be difficult with close relatives when you tell them you are standing on the word of God for your healing, and they know you have have been told you have only a few years to live. They don't understand that.

When I went for the examination my original doctor was not in so I saw one of his associates. He performed an examination, and then he checked my medical history and said: "Mr. Shaffer, I really cannot explain it, but obviously something has happened to you. The person whose records I am looking at and the person standing in front of me are two different people. You don't need heart surgery now and you probably never will."

My healing was gradual. I wasn't really aware of it as it was happening. Every symptom left, but there were a couple of recurrences. One of them was on the first anniversary of the time I took my stand to be healed by the word of God. On one of the tapes I listened to it was stated when you set your faith to receive your healing lock on to it. Declare: "it is 2:30 in the afternoon of February 10th and I receive my healing now by faith."

It was one year from the day I declared my healing that satan tried to put the symptoms of heart disease back on me. The Bible says that it is satan who has come to steal, kill and destroy. The attack lasted for several days, but by then I was not ignorant of satan's devices. I knew how to use my faith and the word of God, to regain my health. I ignored the symptoms. I did not dwell on them. I did not give them my attention. I kept confessing my healing. I kept confessing the word of God concerning me. The symptoms soon left. I went back to jogging and building up my body.

On February 10th of 1987 I celebrated the fifth anniversary of my healing. I had not died or even weakened. I had gained strength. I said: "God, I am alive, and glad to be alive. Thank You."

*   *   *

" I sought the Lord, and he heard me, and delivered me from all my fears." Psalm 43:4

"I would have lost heart, unless I had believed that I would see the goodness of the Lord in the land of the living. Wait on the Lord. Be of good courage, and He shall strengthen your heart."
                                                   Psalm 27:13-14

          *   *   *

"The words of the Lord are pure words, like silver tried in a furnace of earth, purified seven times. You shall keep them, O Lord, You shall preserve them from this generation forever."
                                                   Psalm 12:6-7

          *   *   *

"Meditate within your heart on your bed, and be still...offer the sacrifices of righteousness, and put your trust in the Lord."   *Psalm 4:4-5*

          *   *   *

"O Lord, my God, I cried out to You, and You have healed me. O Lord, You brought my soul from the grave..."   *Psalm 30:2-3*

Robert Denning

*"Therefore I say to you,
whatever things you ask, when
you pray, belive that you receive
them, and you will have them."
Mark 11:24*

I was born into a Christian home, and as a boy I attended church every Sunday. I believe that I understood parts of the gospel at that time, but as I grew older I turned away from the church. I felt that I had to have control of my own life, and I had no need of a savior. I felt like many people do, that I had plenty of time to get my life together when the time came, preferably at the end of my life, or as close to the end as possible. I felt that way right up to the time I was diagnosed as having multiple sclerosis.

At that time there wasn't much going right in my life. My business was not in good shape. It was up and down, the way most non-Christian businesses are. We had timber properties at that time, and a saw mill. The economy was lousy. There were problems at home. Basically, I was the problem. Then came the MS.

The first symptoms came five years before I was diagnosed. At that time I thought I had a stroke because I had considerable numbness on the left side of my body. All the doctor could tell me was that I did not have a stroke, and that there were several diseases which had the symptoms I was exhibiting. I didn't go to a doctor again for five years.

Later I learned that MS normally attacks in two stages. First there is the minor attack such as I had, and then some time later it comes back in full force. It depends on the individual. It was in 1980 the disease hit me with full force. I became completely incapacitated. I couldn't walk or feed myself. I couldn't go to the bathroom by myself, or even focus my eyes. My mind was still clear, however, and I could hear. That was about it.

I was in and out of the hospital a good deal, and steadily going down hill. I was a real problem to my family because I needed so much care. The doctors wanted to try experimental treatments, including radiation, but they told me I was going to die. There is no known treatment for MS, and they said I had about five years to live from the onset of the severe symptoms, and I had used up much of those five years already.

I had to be carried to the doctor's office for my appointments, and I had noticed a growing sadness in his eyes with each visit. He had no good news to tell me. MS is a very debilitating disease. It attacks the nerves, and you have no control. I was almost forty years old, and my facial muscles sagged so I looked like I was sixty. I felt I was trapped inside a dying body.

Then an amazing thing happened. Scriptures which I had learned as a boy began to come back to me, even though my body was in total collapse. I started communicating with the Lord. A peace began to come over me. I had great mental comfort. I knew that I was saved; that I had come back to the Lord. My family started praying for my healing.

I told the doctors that I didn't want any more of the experimental treatments. I began to sense that God was going to heal me. The doctor said to me: "Bob, you have to do something. You have to make preparations. You are dying. You are going to have to sell your business and make some preparations for your family." He told me there was no hope. There was nothing he could do for me.

It was at that time my wife and daughter heard Kenneth Copeland, a Bible teacher on tv, and he was teaching things none of us had heard before. They got all excited about it, and they sent off for some of his teaching tapes. My wife got a cassette tape player and put it on the pillow next to my head and played those tapes to me.

At first I thought the man was a fanatic. If I could have moved my arms I would have grabbed the tape player and thrown it out the window, but I was paralyzed. The only thing that worked on me was my hearing. I lay there and listened to those tapes because there was nothing else I could do, but I didn't believe a thing Copeland was teaching. I didn't see how anyone could believe the blind could see and the deaf could hear.

By this time I was spending the greater part of my waking hours in prayer. I felt that my family was going through a lot of suffering because of me. I was praying: "Lord, I am not of use to anyone around here, and I would really like to come home and be with You unless You have something better for me here." That was when it was revealed to me in my spirit to ask for my healing, and to accept it.

I started *really* listening to those tapes. I had honestly thought that Kenneth Copeland was just a religious fanatic. Then one night, just before I received my healing, I was in prayer. I was in a good place spiritually. Suddenly in the middle of that prayer time I realized that I no longer thought of this man as a fanatic. I had become just like him. My attitude was just like his.

"You don't have to be sick," Kenneth would say, and he would refer to Mark 11:23-24. I listened to the tapes over and over again and Mark 11:23-24 began to become very real to me. Those verses tell us to command the mountain to move. My mountain was multiple sclerosis. I commanded it to move out of my body, and I commanded satan to get out of my affairs.

I spoke to my legs. I called them strong, because the Bible tells us to call thing that be not as though they are. I declared my healing, and I said I would walk. I praised God for my healing.

The next morning I was able to get partially out of bed. It was obvious to me that I had more strength than I had the day before. I commanded my legs to walk, in the name of Jesus. They walked. They walked wobbly, but they walked. I had not been able to walk for a year and a half. I got dressed by myself. That was a very big thing. It took a long time, but I got dressed, and with two people supporting me, I went to my office.

I only worked for about ten minutes that first day. With MS you sleep most of the time. I would doze off. But, that first day I had about ten minutes of mental clarity, and I worked. Then they took me home, and for the rest of the day I confessed my healing. The next day I had them take me back to the office and I put in a good, solid fifteen minutes of work. I had to be assisted up and down the steps, but within two weeks I was walking those stairs by myself and working eight hours a day.

I didn't look so good. People who would see me on the

street at that time would tell me I should get to a hospital. I didn't look good at all. My body was still a mess. I looked like an old man who was dying, but inside I knew better.

I would tell them I had all of the help I needed. I had Jesus. I told them I was healed, and I was being blessed. Everything began working right. I went back to see the neurologist who had been treating me. The last time I had seen him he told me there was no point in my coming to his office anymore because I was going to die and there was nothing he could do for me. When he saw me he could not believe what had happened. I told him it was Jesus. He was amazed.

I believe that Jesus took our sickness at the cross. The Bible says that. So there is no reason for us to be sick. The Bible says that we perish because of a lack of knowledge. If you know the word of God, you can receive your healing. It took about three weeks for my total healing to become manifested. I have not had a recurrence, nor will I ever have one.

*   *   *

"...whatever things are true, whatever things are noble, whatever things are pure, whatever things are lovely, whatever things are of good report, if there is any virtue and if there is anything praiseworthy; meditate on these things."
Philippians 4:8

"Now this is the confidence we have in Him, that if we ask anything according to His will, He hears us. And if we know that He hears us, whatever we ask, we know that we have the petitions that we ask of Him "
I John 5:14-15

*   *   *

"Uphold me according to Your word, that I may live, and let me not be ashamed of my hope"
Psalm 119:116

*   *   *

"Blessed is the man who makes the Lord his trust."
Psalm 40:4

Katherine Scott
(age 12)

"He shall call upon Me, and I will
answer him; I will be with him in
trouble: I will deliver him and
honor him. With long life I will
satisfy him, and show him my
salvation." Psalm 91:14–16

Teddy Scott (Katherine's mother)

The terrible accident happened on July 23rd, 1986, the wedding day of Prince Andrew and Sarah Ferguson. Our girls, Katherine, 12, and Laura, 14, wanted to see the pageantry, and specially the horses and carriages. The whole family got up early to watch the satellite tv broadcast from England.

After watching the telecast the girls went to the barn, about two blocks from our Pensacola home, to feed their horses. While I was making the beds and John was getting ready for work the phone rang. It was Laura and she was very upset. She said: "Mom, quick, get Dad over here. Fred just kicked Katherine in the head." Fred was Laura's horse.

I told John to just forget about putting on his shoes and to quickly get down there and see what happened. He was very calm. He normally is. He finished getting dressed, and then left. I hurriedly dressed and followed him. It was about 8 a.m., and all of our neighbors had already left for work.

As I headed for the pasture Laura and a girl who worked at the barn came around the corner and picked me up. John had taken Katherine directly to the hospital in his car, and that is where we headed. I began interrogating Laura right away, which was a terrible thing to do at that time. I realized it was wrong, but I kept asking questions.

"What happened? How could it have happened? Couldn't you have prevented it?" I was distraught. I just couldn't imagine this happening to my little girl. Laura was upset because of the accident and my accusing questions. She just kept telling me what Katherine looked like and how she had a big hole in the middle of her forehead and how her brain was showing and that brain tissue was out on her face.

Suddenly, in the midst of this turmoil, I experienced one of the most real things that ever happened to me. It wasn't an audible voice. I heard it deep down inside of me: "Just be quiet. Don't say another word. Don't ask any questions. Just read the 91st Psalm."

John Scott (Katherine's father)

After Laura phoned that Katherine had been kicked in the head Teddy was upset and kept urging me to just forget about my shoes and get down to her. I didn't have my shirt on either. I wanted to run out of the house, but it was then that all of the things I had been learning in my Bible study and from anointed faith teachers began to come to the forefront.

One of the first things that came to my mind was that the devil always tries to rush you, but the Lord will gently lead you. I refused to be rushed. I didn't dawdle, but I didn't panic and run. I began calling on the Lord. I finished dressing, got in the car, and quickly drove to the field.

When I got there I could hear this terrible screaming as soon as I got out of the car. Laura was bent over Katherine who was laying on the ground. Laura was crying, and Katherine had her hands up in this horrible wound. I couldn't see her face. It was totally obliterated. It was just blood, and there was a pool of blood under her head. There was a gaping hole in her forehead. She had been kicked just above her eyes. There was brain tissue on her face, and she had her hands up in her brain.

I opened my mouth, and out came Psalm 34:20. I spoke it directly to Katherine: "Honey, *He keepeth all of your bones, and not one of them shall be broken." I* didn't say anything else, but I repeated that Psalm over and over, as I picked her up and ran to the car with her. We were about twelve miles from the hospital, and it seemed the Lord opened the way for us. Even though it was morning rush hour we were not delayed. The traffic just opened up before us.

On the way I held Katherine with one hand and drove with the other. She was in the reclining passenger seat. I remembered Kenneth Copeland teaching on spiritual combat and saying that when the bully (satan) comes to your house to intimidate you and steal your property, it is too late then to start a body building program.

We had gotten on the word of God in 1976 when we were facing another very serious medical situation in our family. At that time I just happened to turn on a radio and heard Kenneth Copeland for the first time as he taught the uncompromising word of God. The things we learned turned that situation around.

Now scriptures were coming to me to meet this circumstance. The things I had been learning about the power of the tongue went off in my spirit like a rocket. They are still going off in my spirit. They have never stopped.

I knew it was critical that I allow only words to come out of my mouth that I desired to come to pass. As I held Katherine's hands to keep her from reflexively putting them into the wound, I talked to her. All the way to the hospital I spoke healing scriptures to her: "Honey, *Jesus bore your sickness and He carried your disease, and by His stripes you are healed.*"

The moment we got to the hospital the medical team went into action. They brought a stretcher and took her from the car, and wheeled her straight to the emergency room. People began running from everywhere; doctors, technicians, nurses. They were doing everything they could to stop the flow of blood and determine the extent of the injury.

Teddy Scott

When Laura and I got to the hospital they already had Katherine in the emergency room. People were streaming in from all the departments. I am a registered nurse, and I worked at that hospital part time. I had been in that emergency room many times. When John saw us he came to me and said: "Don't go in there. Don't look at her. Just don't. I don't want you to see her."

I could see the wisdom of how John was handling it. He wanted my faith to be strong. He didn't want my mind cluttered with the "facts." Being a nurse I would tend to rely strongly on my medical knowledge. John wanted at that moment for me to see her exactly as she had been the last time I was with her, which was normal and healthy.

Laura phoned our pastor. She was by then very calm and very cool. She said: "Please come to the hospital. Katherine has been hurt, and mom wants you to come and read the 91st Psalm to her."

While Laura was phoning I could hear Katherine in the emergency room. She was screaming at the top of her lungs. I kept thinking this was a good sign. She was alive and fighting. You could hear her all over the hospital.

I remember going over and sitting down by the phone booth, and a hospital security guard came to me and asked if I were a patient. I told him I was just trying to concentrate. I kept thinking it would be good if I could just get away from there and not have to see all those people scurrying around and not have to hear Katherine.

I began to speak and call things that be not as though they are. I asked the guard for a Bible, and he said he didn't have one. I asked him to please go to a patient room and get one for me. He was wonderful. He ran and got a Bible for me.

I started to read the 91st Psalm, and I put Katherine's name in every verse. John stayed in there with Katherine while they worked on her. Several of our friends arrived with our pastor. They went in to Katherine and anointed her with oil, according to the Bible.

The doctors came out and told me they were calling in a neurosurgeon, and an eye, ear, nose and throat specialist because her sinuses, eyes and orbits were affected. They were calling in a plastic surgeon. They told me her brain was exposed.

While my mind was trying to take all of this in scriptures were coming up in my spirit. "He gives His angels charge over Katherine to keep her in all of her ways." They took us to a little room off the waiting room while they were gathering the surgical team. I just kept reading the 91st Psalm over and over. I had told the pastor to go in to Katherine and read the 91st Psalm to her. He said: "Sure." It was as if he had knowledge then that she was going to be alright. By that time there were four ministers there, and our family friend, Tom. They were all with Katherine, but I didn't go in.

Reports of Katherine's condition began to spread through the hospital. "This is bad...she might not make it...if she lives her brain is gone...she is blind...she will never be able to see...prepare the parents...help them to understand what brain damage is." It just went on and on. They kept her in the emergency room for three hours while they were assessing the damage, gathering the surgical team, and taking emergency measures to stabilize her for surgery.

As she was taken to surgery men of God from all over the area were gathering at the hospital. Prayer chains were activated all over the city. We began to receive phone calls from as far away as Indiana and South Carolina. Christian friends called just to let us know they had heard about Katherine and they were praying.

So, there we were, hearing from the medical staff on the one hand how devastating this accident was, and then hearing from Christian friends that they were standing with us on the promises of God's word. We knew we had a choice. We knew that God's word says: *"I place before you this day blessings and cursings, life and death, therefore, choose life so that you and your seed after you shall live."* We had the medical opinion on one hand and the word of God on the other. We chose life. We never once let go of our confession that Katherine would live and declare the works of the Lord.

John Scott

Before she was taken to surgery several ministers and myself gathered around Katherine in the emergency room. We anointed her with oil in the name of the Lord Jesus Christ. We prayed the prayer of faith over her, and we read the 91st Psalm as Teddy had been instructed to do: *"I will say of the Lord, He is my refuge and my fortress; my God, in Him will I trust...surely He shall deliver thee from the noisome pestilence...there shall be no evil befall thee, neither shall any plague come nigh thy dwelling. For He shall give His angels charge over thee, to keep thee in all thy ways. They shall bear thee up in their hands, lest thou dash thy foot against a stone...he shall call upon Me and I will answer him...I will be with him in trouble; I will deliver him, and honor him. With long life will I satisfy him, and show him My salvation."*

Teddy Scott

It was a long six hours while Katherine was in surgery. When they finished they didn't sound optimistic. They told us they had repaired the wound as best they could, but they could give us no guarantees. They said they had to remove a lot more brain tissue than they had originally thought because it was so damaged. One doctor told us it was the worst kind of an accident because it happened in a barnyard where there are all sorts of germs which can cause terrible infections that are extremely hard to combat.

We were told that because of the brain injury she was likely to develop a very violent personality. They didn't know about her eyes, but they said she could be blind, and that if she were not blind she probably would not be able to focus her eyes because the muscles and nerves in that area were so badly damaged. Her eyelids were turned inside out, and they were swollen shut. When we went into the intensive care unit to see her after surgery she was just pitiful looking.

She was lying there quietly, and I went to her and told her how much I loved her. I knew that it was all up to God because there was nothing humanly we could do to help her. She was very alert. She couldn't see. Her head had been shaved. She had a big dressing. When we left the ICU the doctor told us again: "I just don't have anything to tell you at this point." He said it was a massive injury, and they had done the best they could with it. I remembered then that when the children were small I would tell them: "Laura and Katherine, you are taught of the Lord, and great shall be your peace and composure." That is Isaiah 54:13.

As I looked back at Katherine in that hospital bed I said: "Lord, You are going to have to guide her and lead her and comfort her." They would only let us be with her for ten minutes every four hours. I asked God to send His angels to be there with her when we could not.

The day after the accident Katherine became very restless. She didn't understand where she was. Her hands were tied down, and she couldn't see. A doctor tried to look at her eyes and check her vision, but he couldn't get any sense from her about whether she could see or not. He said he would try again in a few days.

Dozens of our friends came to us, and they were just wonderful. They would ask how she was, and I would answer them with scripture: "She is going to live and declare the works of the Lord. God made her. He is the author and the finisher." I would see in my mind someone building a house. First one person would come and do the rough work, and then the finisher would come and cut the special pieces of wood and fit them in amazing ways to finish the house. I saw the doctors had completed the rough work, and now the Finisher was going to come and heal my daughter.

We had taken many anointed tapes to the hospital to play for Katherine. One of the music tapes was by Bill Gaither called My Father's Angels. When we played that tape for her she would calm down and lay there quietly holding my hand and listening and I could talk to her. The lyrics told how even on the darkest night, when she couldn't see, the angels could see her, and they were there whether she could see them or not.

We told her over and over how much God loved her. One day I told her: "Katherine, Momma loves you so much, but God loves you so much mores than I do, so much more than we can even imagine, and He is here with you when I cannot be."

They told us it would be a long, long recovery. She was in the neuro intensive care unit. Her personality was different. She was very hostile, but as I began to pray I came to realize this was a good sign, not a bad sign. She was combative, but she knew when it was a nurse touching her or one of the family. When I entered the room she knew me, and she would say: "Hi, Mom." But she didn't want the nurses to be around her. I began praying they would move her from ICU to a private room so we could be with her. Then we could play Bible tapes to her, read the word of God to her, and pray with her.

On the sixth day after the accident she was moved to a regular room. From that day until she was discharged we didn't leave her. One of us was with her all the time. Her progress from that point was dramatic. We could be with her, touch her, feed her, help her.

The day she came out of ICU she was very frustrated because she couldn't see. It was a test of faith for me too because I didn't know if her eyes were working or not. They were swollen shut. She got very loud and she said: "Momma, I want to see." She cried and big tears came out of her eyes, but she couldn't open them. She said: "Momma, I want to see, and I can't see anything."

I told her: "Katherine, you can see. Your face is swollen. Take your fingers and lift your eye lids and look." She did that. Her eyes were terribly blood shot. She took one look around, let out a big sigh, and then lay back on her pillow and went to sleep. I knew she could see. I just knew God had fixed her eyes. Later an ophthalmologist examined her and she has 20/20 vision. Her eyes focus perfectly.

She was very positive. Soon she was up and walking the corridors of the hospital visiting patients. She became the old Katherine. She would walk up to people and say: "Do you think I am a boy or a girl?" Her hair hadn't started to grow back yet, and she thought it was kind of funny. Before the accident her hair had been down to her waist.

She never once complained of any pain. Never. Once I asked her if she hurt because it seemed so strange she didn't complain after that massive injury. She just said: "No, Mom, I'm fine." I knew God had her in the palm of His hand. Whenever anyone asked her how she was doing she always said: "Fine."

Katherine touched the lives and hearts of many people because those who came to see her knew how awful that accident was. They would see her walking the hospital corridors and knew they were watching a miracle.

We first learned of the power of the word of God, the Bible, through the teachings of Kenneth Copeland. John ordered a number of little prayer cards from Copeland's ministry, and one based on the 91st Psalm was for children. That prayer became very meaningful to me. When something as overwhelming as Katherine's accident comes into your life you go on automatic pilot. Your brain stops working and your spirit takes over. Whatever is in your spirit comes out.

I had the 91st psalm in my spirit. Your mind wants to go crazy, but your spirit turns to the scriptures you have planted in your heart, and your faith comes rushing to apply itself to the problem. Several times my nurse's mind came to the forefront, but I kept turning to my spirit. In the car on the way to the hospital my nurse's mind kept telling me: "Now, you are going to have call in this specialist and that specialist."

But out of my spirit came the realization of the importance of the 91st Psalm. That psalm was more important than anything a medical team could do, more important than any intravenous feeding they could start, or any x-ray or surgical procedure.

The 91st Psalm at that time became like a medical procedure to me. It was "doctor's orders." At the time it seemed so obviously the right thing to do. Looking back on it I know that it wasn't just a "good idea" I had at the time. It was the Holy Spirit of God transmitting vital spiritual information to my human spirit. I knew it was not God's will for Katherine to be taken at the age of twelve. It is the devil who has come to kill, steal and destroy.

In the midst of all that trauma and crisis it was God who impressed His will on me. It was never audible, but it was the most real thing I have ever experienced. When I was quizzing Laura in the car on the way to the hospital I was just drilling her. I just couldn't imagine how this could have happened, and God told me to just be quiet. It didn't matter how it happened. My focus turned from accusation to: "We've got to fix this." I knew the way to fix it was with the word of God, the scriptures. I've come to know that no matter what has happened you must not give up, and you have to depend on the word of God.

Any time you find yourself in a situation where you have no answers, the 91st Psalm is your answer. Many doubts assailed me. My nurse friends would tell me medical "facts" that would shake my faith. We didn't sleep much those first few weeks. We stayed right at the hospital and when we weren't with Katherine we listened to faith-building Bible teaching tapes and we read our Bibles.

I would go in to look at her and after the first week the cranial fluids from around her brain began to drain directly onto her face. It would be all over her pillow and sheets, and my nursing knowledge would come to me and I would think, how are they ever going to prevent her from getting a meningitis infection. The air is full of germs, and her with that open wound.

John would say: "I'm not worried. God has it under control." He was like a rock, but I'd sometimes waver. I would spend a little time around the doctors and the nurses, and then come back to John and say: "How do you think Katherine's color is?" He would say: "I'm not concerned with her color. God is in control of her color and her brain. He made her." The mother's heart is just different from the father's heart.

When I told John I was afraid I was wavering in my faith because of all I was seeing and hearing, he told me: "Don't be concerned about wavering in your mind. That is just the devil hitting your mind. Don't waver in your heart. Just keep putting the word of God in your heart, and concentrate on keeping your heart steady. Your mind will be bombarded, but if your heart is established it will not waver."

I began to see some things then. I figured the devil was hitting me so hard night and day with this thing that there must be something wonderful about to happen. There must be a real victory on the horizon or he wouldn't be so busy trying to convince me of how bad things are. I had heard a lot about wavering before, but when you are in the trenches you learn all about it.

John Scott

Those first few days it was as if the devil had one of those flip charts salesmen use. He would flip a page and show us: "She is so badly injured she cannot live." We would answer that with the word of God: "Katherine shall live and declare the works of the Lord." The devil would flip to the next page: "She has lost so much brain tissue that she will have severe brain damage and personality problems." We would counter with the scripture: "She has the mind of Christ." Satan flipped to page three: "She is blind." We didn't buy that one either. But he just kept assaulting us in our minds; just kept flipping those pages, giving us one devilish diagnosis after another trying to find the one we would accept and set our faith on. We didn't buy any of them. Teddy and I just kept confessing that by Jesus' stripes Katherine was healed.

Katherine had just finished seventh grade when she was kicked, and in the fall she was to start a new school. After the accident they tested her scholastic ability, and she was above grade level. She had no brain damage. No matter how negative the reports, we just stood on the word of God and watched as He turned things around. Katherine was a real trooper through it all. She never complained, except for the time her eyes were swollen shut and she couldn't see. She was never in pain.

When she began mending she bugged the doctors about riding again. "When can I ride my horse again? Doctor, as soon as I get out of here I want to ride my horse" She really worked on them. She has a lot of guts. Many people didn't think she would live. When she did live, they didn't think she would ever get back on a horse again.

One of her doctors told me that if it were her daughter he would never let her ride again. We did give the matter some consideration. If it had been left totally up to me, without any concern for Katherine's wishes, I would have told her not to ride anymore. But, I knew that God was able to protect and keep Katherine. God didn't cause that accident. We cannot explain why things happen, but we know that through it all God was there. He brought her through, and He will always bring her through, no matter what the circumstance. Katherine pointed out to me that she wasn't kicked while riding her horse. She loves to ride, and we couldn't take that away from her.

Teddy Scott

Of course I had mixed feelings about Katherine riding again. I am not a horse person. Part of me didn't want her back on a horse ever again. I thought another accident could happen. The devil used that. He uses fear to get into our affairs. I realized those kind of feelings could plague me for the rest of my life if I gave in to them.

I did not want to go against the doctor's advice. I looked on the doctor as her authority in this situation. I wanted those doctors to be in agreement that it would be alright for her to ride. I didn't want any strife or confusion about it.

When Katherine came home from the hospital friends came and taught her cross stitch and bread making. When she was doing cross stitch she would say: "I'll sure be glad when this is done so I can get back to the barn." Friends took her sightseeing, to football games, and school activities, but all she would talk about was her horse.

She waged a regular campaign with her doctors to get their permission. The main man she had to convince was the neurosurgeon, and she began writing notes to him. She explained how safe her pony was, and that it wasn't her horse that kicked her; it was her sister's horse. She reminded him over and over the accident hadn't occurred while she was riding. She had been standing in the pasture when she was kicked. She told the doctor she knew she could do it, and that it was a desire of her heart.

She told her father she felt it was God's will to let her ride. She had gotten five doctors to agree with her, but the neurosurgeon was the holdout. Finally, he gave in. He said that if Katherine was his daughter he wouldn't let her ride again, but if she wanted so badly to ride to let her. He told her to always wear a hard hat.

Katherine entered the first horse show on the schedule which was December 8, 1986. It was just after Thanksgiving the doctor had given his permission, and she hadn't ridden in months.She was only able to ride a few times before the show. She did get in a few lessons, and the teacher was concerned if her muscles were firm enough.

It rained for days before the show, so she didn't get in more than two hours of riding. The day of the show she was up at daybreak. She had everything laid out. She had made a list of everything she was to take to the show. We got to the show grounds at 6 a. m. Her event was scheduled for 11 a. m.

Sixteen people were entered in her class. They were all good athletes, and they had been practicing for weeks. She had been out of action for months with a severe head injury. It didn't look like she stood any sort of chance of placing.

We stood with all her friends at the fence watching. Katherine was so intent. It was as if she were the only person out there. She didn't look around. She concentrated on the commands and on her riding. Everyone on the sidelines was calling out the names of the various riders who were doing well, and who they thought would place.

When they announced the awards Katherine had forgotten her number, which was pinned to her back. She hadn't looked at it all day. They called her number several times, and then called her name for the blue ribbon. She had won first place.

That was the most wonderful moment. It wasn't the blue ribbon itself. It was that God had restored her completely. He had answered all of our prayers. She was better than before the accident. Her trainer told us later that she had some bad riding habits before she was kicked, but she had worked them all out.

I saw the spiritual lesson in that. If we will just do our little teeny part; and our part is just to listen to the word, God makes it so simple. He has laid it all out for us. He tells all the things He will do for us if we will just believe and not doubt. It may not sound logical, and at times it may not sound sensible, but if we will just believe Him we will see the glorious result.

As I watched her in that show ring I thought, God is so good. He not only gave us back our daughter, He made her new, and He loves her so much that He has given her the desire of her heart. She didn't have to be content to do counted-cross-stitch which is probably last on her list of favorite hobbies. He enabled her to do the thing she loves most in the world, and He let her excel at it.

If she gave up horses tomorrow it wouldn't bother me. I am just thrilled that whatever she wants to do God has restored her so that she is physically able to do it. She's perfect. The first part of the 1986 school year Katherine was in home school. I have her report cards from that six week period. She made straight A's. She learned by tape recorder and phone and it wasn't the most ideal learning situation.

Through all these circumstances God kept reminding me that He made the universe, and He can fix any situation. As a mother I learned that I can trust more than I ever thought possible. It became so real to me that we love our children in deeper ways than we have imagined. If they even get a splinter it bothers us. How much more must the compassion of God be to give up His Son who is perfect for we who are imperfect. How it must have hurt Him to know He was going to have to face Calvary so that Katherine could be healed. It was a very revealing six months for me, and I will never be the same.

Katherine is just very normal now. There is no residual from the accident. Her first day back at school she ran 36 laps; something over three miles. She was six weeks behind her class and she tried to catch up in one day. We cannot see any problems. There is a slight scar on her forehead. Her personality is fine.

She has always had a servant's heart. She had been home from the hospital about a month when she came into our room one night and said: "Would you like me to get you a drink of water or something? I just thought you might be thirsty." That is her nature.

When the accident first happened I knew that if I let my mind wander, and listened to everything the medical staff was saying, that I would be a basket case. I made up my mind I was going to read the 91st psalm until I saw victory. I would read it constantly. For six months if necessary. I sat in that emergency room while they worked on Katherine, and I read it over and over and over. The Bible says to not let the word depart from our eyes, but to keep it before us. I made up my mind that day I would not let the scriptures depart from my eyes.

We brought teaching tapes on faith and healing to the hospital. We played them for Katherine, and we listened to them ourselves at every opportunity. Whenever anything would happen to shake my faith, and I could feel myself sliding into doubt, I would quickly find John, and have him pray with me and encourage me. I determined I was not going to entertain doubt and unbelief. We are surrounded by it in the world, but we don't have to accept it.

Katherine had many wonderful doctors and nurses, but I knew it was going to be the word of God that healed her. The scriptures say that He sent His word to heal us. We were always in the word, reading our Bibles, praying, listening to anointed teaching tapes, building each other up. The scriptures make you strong when you are weak. When you are exhausted the scriptures will energize you.

I learned that when you hear God saying it, you can put your faith in it. He said that with long life He will satisfy us and show us His salvation. I remember thinking as I read that from my Bible: "Hey, God said that. Who am I to make *any* comment on it."

John Scott

I had a peace right from the start. I knew all would be well. I know that faith comes by hearing, and hearing by the word of God. In 1976 I was listening to my car radio and heard Kenneth Copeland teach on our confession of faith. I immediately sent for all of his teaching tapes, and as a family we discovered the word of God is truly God's word, and that when you hear it, and act on it, God will do what He has said He will do.

God has told us that satan was overcome by the blood of the Lamb (Jesus Christ) and the word of our testimony. Jesus did His part by shedding His blood. In the simplicity of the word, all I have to do is add the word of my testimony to the shed blood and then step back and watch the results in my family's life.

In 1977 we attended Kenneth Hagin's Camp Meeting in Tulsa, and from that meeting we brought back a teaching series on faith. I listened to them so much I had them memorized. The word is in us. It has built us up. It is in our children. I taught a Bible class for three years based on what I learned from those faith tapes.

December 8th, 1986 was the culmination for me. That was the day Katherine won the blue ribbon at the horse show. Her mother said that if Katherine had been riding a donkey that day she would have won because victory was coming from deep inside her.

When she was presented with the ribbon her friends were sobbing and crying. So were her mom and dad. They all knew the odds she was battling, but the judges didn't know. It was just a wonderful day. Every thing was back to normal. Everything was back the way it should be. Satan had been defeated again, and faith had won. It was exceedingly abundantly above anything we could have asked or thought.

*   *   *

*" I have set the Lord always before me;
because He is at my right hand,
I shall not be moved. Therefore my heart
is glad and my glory rejoices; my flesh
also shall rest in hope." Psalm 16:8-9*

Helen Costanza

"God has not givien us a spirit of
fear, but of power, and of love and
of a sound mind." II Timothy 1:7

The Lord has performed a miracle in my life. Sometimes I just stand back and look on with amazement. I am at a loss for words. I feel no one can understand how hard I fought this battle and how hopeless it seemed. I have tried many times before to put this down on paper and found myself in tears while going over the memories.

I was not raised in a Christian home, but I always had a great desire to know God. I grew up in the midst of a lot of fighting and no real love. At the age of 18 I left home, got pregnant and then got married. We had two children in the three years we were married, and then we divorced.

I guess I left home to get married and be loved and have children so that I could love them with the love I didn't get when I was growing up. I soon remarried, and my daughters were my life. I loved them so much. I wanted to give them a good home, and I did, and things worked out well for a time.

I never felt I was good enough, and I let people walk all over me and abuse me. Starting when I was 14, four times Christians told me about Jesus, but I rejected them each time.

Then one day a girl came to my home and we talked. She was a Christian. She told me that she had been praying for me, and she had a vision of my praising the Lord. I did not understand what she was talking about, but I could not forget the things she told me.

I accepted the Lord then. I knew it was what I wanted, and I loved it. Two days later I was baptized in the Holy Spirit. From that day on I had a great desire to lay hands on the sick and pray for them as the Lord told us to do. It was a strong desire. I would see people in wheelchairs, and it would make me mad. I really cannot explain that, but I knew people do not belong in wheelchairs.

Two months later I was told I had cancer. At that time I could not even begin to believe the Lord for healing. I did not know a thing. I had only been saved for two months. I was operated on, and the surgeon told me they were able to remove all of the cancer.

It was after that the big problems started. We moved to Chicago where the only people I knew were my husband's family. I attended church for a time. My husband's family did not like me. When I had gotten saved I had stopped doing the things I used to do, and they disliked me even more. They would come over to our home and get drunk and laugh at me. They would take my husband out, and I would stay home. It wasn't long before they pulled me away from church and back into their world. I was not strong enough to resist the pull of the world. But, I was not happy in that life. I had the Lord, and I knew I was doing wrong. I had a little bit of God, and a little bit of the world, and I was confused.

Things began to get worse for me. One day I was sitting on the floor of the living room playing with my girls when I heard a voice say: "KILL THEM."

I was scared. Very scared. When my husband got home I told him, and he just said:"Oh, come on, now, Helen." I tried to put it out of my mind. A few days later I heard the voice again: "YOU ARE NOT A GOOD CHRISTIAN. THE LORD DIDN'T SAVE YOU. JUST LOOK AT YOURSELF."

I did not know what was happening to me. As time went on things got worse. I went to different churches and told them about the voices. They said it was a demon talking to me. They told me to believe that Jesus would take it away. They laid hands on me, but it did not go away. At one church they took me into a room and prayed. I vomited after they ordered the demon to come out. It still was not gone. I had no faith, and I could not understand what they were talking about.

Then I went to see a doctor to see if he could help. He said I was crazy, and he put me on some pills that only confused me more. It got worse. Then I began to have weird thoughts: "YOU CAN'T STAY ALONE WITH YOUR CHILDREN. YOU WILL KILL THEM." I would go driving in a car, and I would hear: "JUMP OUT." It got to the point where I could not stay alone with my girls. I would make my husband stay with me. I was scared, and I could not understand why I was hearing voices and thinking these weird thoughts. Also, I was getting physically sick.

I could not understand how these things could be happening to a Christian. The voice said: "YOU ARE NO GOOD. YOU ARE A DOG. BARK LIKE A DOG." It sounds nuts, but it really happened. I believe that some of it could be traced to the pills I was taking, but I was also beginning to think I really was crazy. I did not yet have any idea it was satan. I thought I had lost my mind. I went to a hospital and they gave me more pills. I felt a little better, and I was discharged and went home. I was spending $71 a week on pills. I just could not understand why, after I got saved, I would get cancer and go crazy. I still could not be alone with my daughters. If I had to be alone in the house with them I would go to a separate part of the house. I was so scared. I loved them, and I was hearing: "YOU ARE GOING TO KILL YOUR GIRLS. SEE, YOU ARE CRAZY." I just could not figure it out.

I told my husband that I had to put my girls where they would be safe, somewhere away from me. I called a friend and asked her if she and her husband could take them until I was better. I told her that I didn't know what was wrong, but I wanted them to be safe. She agreed to take them, but she said I would have to give her legal custody of them until they were 18. I did not like to do that, but I wanted them safe, so I signed the papers. My husband told me that if he were their real father he would throw me in a ditch somewhere and take the girls away with him. He took me to my mother's house and left me there, and he took off for California.

With my girls safely at the friend's house I believed those thoughts and voices would stop. But, I had no sooner gotten to my mom's house than I heard: "KILL HER." I told her:"Mom, I cannot stay here. My thoughts are telling me to kill you." She was crying when I left. She didn't want to know what was happening to me. I went to another friend's house and stayed there for a while. I would just lay on the bed all day. I was taking ten pills a day. My husband was gone. My daughters were gone. My home was gone. Then I heard: "JUMP OUT THE WINDOW. TAKE THE LAMP CORD AND STRANGLE YOURSELF." I paid my friend to hide the knives where I couldn't find them. I got to the point where I could not be alone by myself. I was scared, confused, lonely and crazy.

When I was in the hospital, before my children left, a doctor had me hold my girls on my lap and then he handed me a butcher knife. He told me if I didn't try to kill them that I was not crazy. I did not hurt the girls. The doctor shook my hand and told me I was not crazy. He said he was convinced I was not crazy. When I went back to that hospital later the doctor told me that he could not help me anymore. He wanted to put me in some psychiatric group home. I told him that I was scared, and that I could not be with people. I was afraid I would kill someone. He told me that he was sure I would not do that because people who do kill do not say they are scared. They just go out of control and do it. He then told me that the only place for me was a mental institution. It was my only hope. I told him that I would go, and if I didn't get better I would just have to stay there for the rest of my life.

I thought I would be safe there, but I wasn't. I could not be around anyone without having thoughts of killing them. I was a very mixed up girl. The first night I went to the staff and asked them if I could be put in a room where I could be alone. I told them that I did not want to kill anyone, and that I might kill myself. They had to get a doctor's order, and they put my in a room where I was tied to a mat on the floor for two days and three nights.

Then they gave me some different pills and let me out of that room. None of the pills worked, and I was put on a long-term ward. They kept trying different pills. They would tell me the new pills were working, but none of them worked. Finally, a doctor said to me: "Why don't you pray to God to help you?"

I didn't act on that advice right away, but as time went on I was out walking on the hospital grounds and what he said came back to me. I had been there for five months by then. I was alone, and I said: "God, please help me." That was all I said. I did not know if He would help me or not. That may sound stupid, but a lot of people had tried to help me and nothing had worked. To me it all seemed hopeless. But, two weeks later I left the hospital. Praise God.

I found out through all of this that man does not have all the answers. Pills didn't work. I ran to everyone except the One I should have gone to in the beginning. He was there all the time. As I was being discharged from that mental hospital my thoughts were: "What are you going to do now?" I had to face the memories of what had happened and go back out in the world and rebuild my life. I was placed in a group home, and I got some help. People let me alone. I had time to read my Bible and pray a lot. I got to talk to my girls. I felt a little better. I kept saying to myself: "I am not going back to that mental hospital."

The Lord began to show me things. I had a little green New International Version of the New Testament in my hand. One of the staff members was sitting with me trying to comfort me. I had thoughts running through my mind like: "The doctors have told me I am crazy. Another doctor told me I wasn't crazy. One said I was just depressed. I'm so confused." Then I just blurted out: "God, am I crazy?" The next thing I heard was a voice saying to me: *"Open the book."*

I had my little Bible on my lap. I opened it, and my eyes fell on the words: *"I AM NOT INSANE."* I was stunned. I said: "Sandy, look." She looked, and then she looked at me, and I at her. I told her that was a word from God. It was the part where Paul was preaching to Festus, and Festus told Paul that his great learning was driving him insane. Paul answered him and said: *"I am not insane."*

God had spoken to me through the Bible. I did not even known those words were in the Bible. The Lord knew it, and I needed to see it. Later he spoke to me again in the same way. Not really thinking, I asked Him when this nightmare was going to end. The Lord led me to Romans 16:20 *"The God of peace will soon crush satan under your feet, and the grace of the Lord will be with you."* Then, in a flash, I knew that all of this was coming at me from satan. It was not from my own mind.

I got into the Bible, and I mean night and day. I was praying in the spirit all of the time. I was required to go to a group therapy session, and I would sit in the corner and read my Bible. They were irritated with me because I wasn't joining in with them, but I was sitting over in the corner being healed by the word of God.

God began to show me from His word that He loved me, and that He would not leave me, and that He was always with me. Everyone else had left me, but the Lord showed me that He would not leave me. My heart was opened. I believed it. It was that simple. I took His word at face value. The more I read the Bible the more the bad stuff left me. I did not understand it then. Everything the Lord said in Psalm 91, such as *"no, evil shall come nigh thy dwelling,"* was right.

I began to understand that the things that had come against me were evil things, and God said it shall not come nigh my dwelling, so I began to believe that, to declare it and to stand on it. I would speak that promise of God out loud, and I would fight the evil thoughts with it. When I did that the evil thoughts and the hurting would fade away and seem unreal. I discovered that His word will not return to Him void, just as it says in the Bible.

As I began to confess the word of God over my circumstances the people around me thought I was really nuts. I did not understand how confessing the word was working, but it was working, and I was getting brave. The light was coming in. I tried to speak only the word of God.

I was getting better, and I knew I had to get out of that home. I had been afraid for so long that I would act on those evil thoughts and voices. Then I found a scripture that said: *"God is faithful who will not let you be tempted beyond what you can bear, but with the temptation will make a way of escape."* I was believing. Now I had to start acting.

My husband had returned from California. He brought my daughters over, and they were going to take me for a ride. I was just joking when I asked him to let me drive the car, but he said that I could. I felt I had to go back and face the memories and the thoughts and confront the terror. When I got behind the wheel I heard: "YOU CAN'T DRIVE. YOU WILL KILL EVERYONE. YOU WILL KILL YOUR KIDS. YOU WILL KILL THEM ALL. YOU ARE CRAZY."

I got scared, just like before, but the next voice I heard said: *"I will never leave you nor forsake you. I am with you always."* I knew that voice. I made a decision then. I could either believe the evil voice, or I could believe God. This was not the "little faith" needed for a pair of socks or the rent money. This was life or death, sink or swim. I realized later that deep, deep, deep down inside of me I believed in God or I would not have driven the car that day. I had acted on what I believed. Then I saw the results as my acting on the word of God overcame the evil. I made it.

The Lord saw me through. He performed His word in me. I shouted out loud: "See, satan, mind, pills, or whatever; THE LORD AND I HAVE DONE IT." When I got back from the ride that day I was by myself when the Lord spoke to me again. He said: *"Perfect love casts out fear."* That is I John 4:18. It had been fear that had been driving me. I finally knew that God loved me. When He gave me His love, and I received it, the fear left. I trusted Him. Gradually the Lord showed me so much more. I kept getting stronger mentally and physically.

It took about seven more months. I faced the fears one at a time. I used the word of God in each instance. I Timothy 1:17 tells me that God has not given me a spirit of fear, but of power and love and a sound mind. Knowing that was a tremendous help to me. Over and over again I told myself that God had said that so it was true. I spoke that scripture aloud over and over again. I called what was not as though it were — according to Romans 4:17 — and today I have a spirit of power and of love and a sound mind.

I wanted my children back, but I had signed them over to my friend until they were 18. My friend did not want to return them. It looked like there was no way to get them back, so I turned again to the Lord. I asked Him to move on the hearts of that family to return my children.

The Lord spoke to me again. He told me to ask and I would receive. That is John 16:24. I had the girls pray that prayer with me, and I got them back, and we are together again. My girl's hurts are all gone, and they are happy again. I just cannot describe how happy I am now. When everyone left me Jesus stayed by my side. He gave me a love beyond understanding. I can now take that love and share it with others. His word is truth, and *"greater is He (Jesus) that is in me than he (satan) that is in the world."*

I realize that to many people this testimony may seem like a small thing, but they weren't there. They didn't have to go through it. I had the fears and the pain and I lost everything and I hurt bad. It is over now and I am strong. I look back now and I cannot even imagine me going through all of that. Through it all I found someone who loves me and He gave me back my life, and He made it much better than it was before.

When I was believing God for deliverance from that bondage I did not know what was happening. Since then I have been studying the Bible in depth and I understand now what was happening. It all fits together now. At the time I was living that nightmare I was scarcely aware of the spiritual dimension of life. I didn't know we had an enemy named satan, and that God has made a way of escape from every trap that enemy sets for us. At the time I was going through that ordeal I trusted no man. They had all failed me. So the Lord took me through it Himself. He did perform His word. There were so many horrible thoughts I had to deal with, but now I am free.

I don't take any pills. I have inner strengths that no one can take from me. I hated what I went through, but I would not take anything for the lessons I learned. At one point I had nothing. Now I have it all back, and so much more.

If you are where I was, I want you to know this. I believe I fought a battle with all the demons of hell. By not understanding back then, with my great desire to serve the Lord, and by playing around with the world, I had caused some of what I went through. But, not knowing this at the time, the Lord looked on my heart, and He had mercy on me.

When I was ready to get help, He was there. I also believe that even when I thought He wasn't there, He really was there. With all the fear I was in, and the voices telling me to do those horrible things, it was God who still held me together and would not let me act on those evil commands.

Jesus gave us life and His word to show us how to live a happy and victorious life. I, with the help of satan, messed it all up, but Jesus with His love and mercy straightened it all out. Without Him I would still be locked up in an institution. What the Lord can give a person is beyond words. He is everything anyone could ask for in life because He is life.

Even though the Lord gave me back my mind, my kids, a home, I think the greatest thing He showed me was His love in us. He gave me that ability to look at a person who will stand there and curse God, a person who, In my mind, I would think is no good, a person I would want nothing to do with, and He lets me see that person through His eyes of love. I hate what they say, but I can still love them, and I believe that is the love the Lord has for each of us.

*   *   *

"He (Jesus) personally bore our sins in His own Body on the tree (as an altar and offered Himself on it) that we might die to sin and live to righteousness. By His wounds you have been healed."
I Peter 2:24

*"And thus He (Jesus) fulfilled what was
spoken by the prophet Isaiah, He Himself
took (in order to carry away) our
weaknesses and infirmities and bore away
our diseases." Matthew 8:17*

*   *   *

*"So shall My word be that goes forth from
my mouth; it shall not return to me void, but it
shall accomplish what I please, and it shall
prosper in the thing for which I sent it."
Isaiah 55:11*

*   *   *

*"You are my hiding place and my shield;
I hope in Your word." Psalm 119:114*

Mike Hall

*"...Death and life are in the power
of the tongue, and they that love it
shall eat the fruit thereof..."*
Proverbs 18:20

My medical problems started in 1977 when I was diagnosed as having Hodgkin's disease. My spleen was removed as part of the treatment. I was 28 years old. The doctors told me that without your spleen it is difficult to fight off bacteria and infections. In 1984 I was working as a coalmine foreman for U.S.Steel, and I also had a maintenance contract for 106 apartment units. I was working hard, involved in lots of things.

I went to bed May 14, 1984 — mother's day — feeling fine, and I awoke at 4 a.m. with hard, shaking chills. I stayed in bed until about 9 a.m. By then I was running a fever, so I got up and took a cool shower to try to knock the fever down. I could hardly stand up. I felt like I was on the verge of blacking out. I knew there was something seriously wrong, so I checked into the local clinic. Within the hour I was taken to our regional hospital.

They gave me a series of tests, and then told me that I had pneumococcal sepsis. They didn't expect me to live through the day. I learned that this is a condition caused by bacteria that usually enter your body through a cut. Normally your body's immune system will combat it, but without my spleen my body couldn't fight back. The first symptoms were a lot like flu.

Four doctors examined me, and they all agreed I wouldn't make it. But God is the one who has the final say. At that time I wasn't even saved, but I had been under conviction for a long time. My wife, Darlene, was saved. She attended church regularly and had been praying for me. She had all of her friends from church praying also. I'd go to church with her every now and then, but I was too proud and independent to take that step and give my life to the Lord. A few hours after I got to the hospital I slipped into a coma. My family were called in, and they all began praying for my recovery. Just about all of our family on both sides are Christians, so there were a lot of folks praying. They got the entire Christian community of Cumberland, Kentucky praying for me. If the gift of faith hadn't been in effect in my wife's life at the time I got sick I do not think I would be around today. She lifted me up spiritually when I couldn't lift myself up. When I was going in and out of the coma I would fight and pray, but it was the prayers of others that got me through the darkest hour.

They couldn't treat me locally. They said I was going to die. My wife insisted I be moved to Saint Joseph's Hospital in Lexington. The doctors said I would not survive the trip, but she arranged for a helicopter to take me that day. She followed by car, and the doctors did everything they could to prepare her to find a dead man when she arrived at Saint Joseph's.

At the hospital they examined me and found I had

developed meningitis and kidney failure. Another complication they found was disseminated intravascular coagulation (D.I.C.) which means that every part of my body was oozing blood, and it was coagulating and cutting down my circulation.

When they took me from the helicopter they thought I was a black man because I had turned dark all over from the clotting of the blood that oozed from my capillaries. Later this caused all of my skin to peel, and the same sort of thing was going on internally as dead tissue was being cast off.

The D.I.C. stopped the circulation in my arms and legs, and that condition was supposed to be as fatal as the pneumococcal sepsis. I was in total kidney failure. I was on a dialysis machine eight hours a day, seven days a week for four weeks.

My wife and I prayed and claimed healing for my kidneys all during that time. After forty days my kidneys began working again. The doctors then said I was in danger of becoming dehydrated because my kidneys were putting out so much. My wife stayed with me in the hospital for 70 of the 76 days I was there.

The Bible says that there is power in prayer when two agree, and my wife and I experienced that. We faced a lot during that ordeal. We learned our lessons on the battlefield. It seemed that after every victory we would find ourselves in another battle. We learned that satan does not give up easily. As soon as I started getting over the pneumococcal sepsis I contracted pseudomonis sepsis which is a related bacteria. That one was also supposed to kill me. Through all of these trials the Lord showed me in different ways that it was Him taking care of me.

Because I had given my life to the Lord at the onset of the

illness, and I had the inner assurance that He had accepted me, I was able to fight effectively in the spirit for my healing. I was at peace inside because I knew from the Bible that if I died I would be with the Lord, so I had no fear to contend with. I didn't want to die. I wasn't preparing to die. I had children to raise, and I loved my family. Also, I wanted to live and do something for Him, and I told Him that in prayer.

This is really hard to explain, and I think it would take someone who has gone through it to really understand it completely, and that is the love with which God filled my heart. I literally felt it. I was born again. The love He gave is just indescribable. Physically I went through a re-birth of sorts also. When I started to heal I peeled from head to toe. The same sort of thing happened internally. I had callouses on my feet and hands built up over years of hard work in the mines, and they just peeled off. The linings of my lungs, stomach, throat, mouth and sinus cavities peeled.

While this was going on I couldn't talk for a while. I couldn't hear. Then everything was new. I even had to learn to sit up and how to walk again. I was just like a baby. God showed me so many things at that time to let me know that He was taking care of me. He showed me that I was going to have to really fight in the spirit to come against all of the physical problems satan was afflicting me with.

No one really knows how I stood against this attack. It seemed like I had my back to the wall, and things were coming at me from everywhere. There was nothing else to do but stand. The only thing that sustained me was the knowledge that God was standing with me, and I knew that because His word says He will never leave us or forsake us.

At one time I had total heart and respiratory failure which was caused by the huge blisters which formed in my lungs.

They had me on a respirator because of the pseudomonis sepsis. The blisters in my lungs got so big the respirator couldn't breath for me, and I couldn't breath for myself. When the blisters broke they filled the tubes of the respirator and I got no air at all. They lost me for about four minutes. They got the tubes out of me, and they got my airways cleaned out, gave me a shot in the heart to get it started again, and I was back among the living.

Twice during my hospitalization they called my family and told them I was gone. There was a man, who I assumed to be the head doctor over that unit, who came in several times and stood either at the foot of my bed or just outside the door. He never examined me, but he was always there when the other doctors examined me, and they would seem to go to him to confer with him about how to best treat me. He would just give them a nod of his head; yes or no. He wore a long white hospital lab coat.

I began to put some dependency in him because he seemed to be the brains over everything that was going on. He came to me twice and spoke to me. The first time was when I had gone into a coma and thought for sure I was dying. He leaned over my bed and said: "I'm going to take care of you." Just as soon as he said that I was out of the coma. My family was all around the bed. The doctor's had called them in because they thought I couldn't live much longer.

My father had his hand on my forehead and was praying. I was told later that as soon as he finished praying and took his hand from my head I awoke from the coma. I suppose the man I took to be the head doctor was my guardian angel or someone sent by the Lord to take care of me.

The second time he talked to me was when I died on that respirator and they lost me for four minutes. I was fighting for breath, and for my life. I struggled for breath as long as I could, and then I thought: "Well, this is it. I can't get any more air." Then I began to get concerned for my family. I wondered what my family would do without me. It was then this man came to me again. He walked up to my bed and put his arm around my shoulder and sat me up and said: "I told you that I am going to take care of you."

As soon as he said that I saw my whole family at the foot of the bed. Everyone was smiling. They were all fine. Then everything got very cool for me. My temperature went down, and my breathing started again. From that point on I got better every day. I never saw that man again. I asked all the hospital staff about him because I wanted to thank him. I still thought he was the head doctor. I described him, but no one knew who I was talking about. When I needed him he was there, but I never saw him again once I was out of danger.

If I could draw well enough I could draw his picture. I still see him clearly in my mind. He was about 5'9" tall in his late fifties or early sixties. He was almost completely bald with a white fringe of hair around the sides and back of his head. He had bushy eyebrows. He had a red, jolly complexion as if he might have had red hair as a young man. His nose was rather large. There was nothing very remarkable about his looks, but I sure had a lot of dependency on him.

After I came out of the coma I began listening to Bible teaching tapes to build up my spirit. Those tapes kept me going at a time when I couldn't read my Bible. I had one arm tied up in the air where the circulation had shut down. I lost a portion of my right arm because of gangrene. The tapes were invaluable in helping me understand the ways of God and how to use the word of God to build up my faith at a time when satan had me in some pretty tough battles.

When you rebuke satan in the name of Jesus, you can just turn around and satan will be right back in your affairs. So many people fight their spiritual battles in a passive way. They don't put their heart in it. They don't rise up in authority and take charge of the situation. To be successful you must get angry and be serious. Run the devil off like you would run a thief out of your home, because that is what he is. There were times in the hospital I had to get violent about it, and stick with it for a long time, before I could feel the oppression lifting.

I have a long list of medical diagnostic terms for the conditions I had. Included were pneumococcal sepsis, meningitis, shock, acute renal failure, metabolic acidosis, seizures, upper gastrointestinal hemorrhage, anemia, heart failure, pseudomonus sepsis, pyloric ulcers, systemic candidiasis, adrenal failure, hepatitis, loss of sight and hearing, and, the Hodgkins disease which was the start of it all.

After my circulation failed my arms and legs were most affected. They called that condition rhabdomyolysis. This caused the gangrene and other complications. I was on life support systems for three weeks. I lost 41 pounds and I was suffering from malnutrition, anorexia, and anemia. After 70 days in the hospital my legs weren't any bigger around than my arms. I couldn't stand up.

The Hodgkins disease is in complete remission. The doctors won't say I am healed, but I have no symptoms. I am in good health. I've gained back the weight I lost. I have good muscle tone. I feel real good. I keep a busy schedule. I'm back in school. I'm doing woodworking and painting. I regularly visit churches and Full Gospel Businessmen's meetings and give my testimony. I don't take any medication.

That sickness put us $200,000 in debt, and we are virtually free from that now.

I would tell anyone who is facing a serious illness to put your trust completely in God. What He says, He will do. He cannot lie. I tell people that if God will do what he did for me, an old coal miner from back in the sticks, He will do it for anyone. When I am asked to intercede in prayer for the sick I always try to get the persons family involved. If it had not been for my family standing by me in prayer when I couldn't help myself, I don't think I would be around today. When you are in pain and with your back against the wall, it is sometimes very hard to maintain your faith. That is when you need the strong faith of your family surrounding and supporting you in prayer.

It takes a childlike faith to get your needed miracle. A child is born without fear or doubt, and he has complete trust. When you become a Christian, and you are reborn, you get a new Father. You can have complete trust in Him with no fear at all. You have to de-program yourself from the world. You have to renew your mind with the word of God. Get in the Bible because faith comes by hearing, and hearing by the word of God.

*   *   *

Sam Perry

"And the whole multitude sought to touch Him (Jesus) for power went out from Him and healed them all." Luke 6:19

My heels first started bothering me in 1977. It developed quickly into a severe problem in both feet. They became tender and very painful. Anytime I would sit still for a few minutes, and then get up and walk, it was extremely painful. But, after a few minutes of hobbling around I would begin to feel well enough that I could walk.

For the first ten minutes after I awoke there was terrible pain in my heels. I would limp around for a time and work it out. It started suddenly, and it quickly developed into continual pain. I do not know of anything I was doing that could have brought it on. It was a condition that I just came to accept. I figured I was going to be like that from then on.

A year or two later I enrolled in graduate school at the University of North Carolina. They had a great sports medicine program, and as a student I would have access to it. One of the first things I did when I got on campus was to make an appointment with the doctors to have my feet examined.

At that time I didn't know the Lord. I thought I did. I'd
been raised in a church where you sort of hoped you were
alright, but you never really knew. We were never shown in
the scriptures where we really stood with God. Our whole
approach was that one day we would stand before Him and
He would weigh the good and the bad that you had done, and
if there was more good than bad then you were saved. That
was the idea I had of salvation.

The doctors at the sports medicine clinic gave me a very
thorough examination. They x-rayed my feet, and several
specialists examined me. I was told that the medical school
there at Chapel Hill had some of the top rated doctors in the
country for problems such as mine, but my condition
stumped them.

They looked at the x-rays, and then said: "Gosh, this is the
strangest looking foot x-ray I have ever seen. I've never seen
bone formation like this. I can see why you are having
problems. This is terrible." They debated among themselves
what it was. They never did give it a medical name, at least
not in my presence. They did rule out things like bone spurs,
and they said it didn't have anything to do with the Achilles
tendon. They did recommend surgery, and a number of
other things. There was a great deal of discussion about what
treatment would be best. They weren't very sure.

I reasoned that if they weren't sure then I certainly was not
going to let them experiment on me. I told them to just forget
the whole thing. Whatever the problem was I would just keep
it.

All of that took place in 1980. Up to that time I had never
heard that we could receive our healing from God, by faith.
A friend had just gotten a set of teaching tapes by Gloria
Copeland on healing, and he loaned them to me.

I was driving my car back from a weekend visit in Statesville. It was a three and a half hour drive and I was alone listening to those tapes. I was hearing that God didn't want me to hobble around half crippled for the rest of my life. He wants me well. He wants me healed. No one had ever told me anything like that before.

Of course Gloria Copeland was giving scripture references from all over the Bible to backup what she was teaching. I was amazed. How come I had never heard any of this before. That teaching was opening up a whole new world to me. I became convinced God wanted me healed. I didn't have any doubts. The Lord just rose up in my spirit and let me know that He was there with me.

Here I was, thirty years old, and He was speaking to my spirit, telling me He didn't want me to be an invalid for the rest of my life. He told me He didn't want me hobbling around on painful feet. He told me that He didn't want me in such a condition that I couldn't run and play with my children.

I was not taking any medication for this condition. One of the doctors had told me take a lot of aspirin because he thought it was some form of arthritis. I took them for a while, but it didn't seem to help so I stopped.

As I listened to those teaching tapes it really struck me: "Hey, this is true. This is God's word. I believe this." I just began to weep over it. I was filled with awe. I didn't do very much crying in those days, but the tears just flowed when that realization came over me. I cried out: "Dear Lord, You love me. You don't want me in this condition." It was such an unexpected revelation to me that God loved me, and that physical disability was not His plan for me.

I went before Him and I began to pray: "Lord, I believe that

You do not want me in this crippled condition. I believe You want me healed." I praised Him and thanked Him, and then it just came all over me: IT IS DONE. IT IS DONE. I drove the rest of the way home praising God all the way.

I was more excited than I had ever been about anything in my life. This was such a revelation to me; that God wanted me healed.

When I stepped out of my car after that three and a half hour drive I felt no pain in my heels whatsoever. It was wonderful. My heels had been so delicate before that I could be wearing a pair of shoes and if you were to take your finger and thump the heel of my shoe — just a gentle thump — it would double me over in pain. It was absolute agony.

Now I began to walk normally and I knew that I was healed. I took one foot and kicked the back of the other. I said aloud: "I'm going to kick it because in the name of Jesus I am healed." I kicked and there was no pain at all. It was absolutely done. I called to my wife. I was so excited. I told her all about it. It was supernatural. After I had decided I was going to have to live with pain for the rest of my life; after the experts in this field of medicine were baffled; then I saw in God's word that I didn't have to suffer, and the pain left me. It was wonderful.

I had no recurrence at all for about two years. Then, one day, for about fifteen minutes, I had a little pain in my heels. I realized what was going on, and I began speaking the word of God concerning my healing. I totally rejected the symptoms, and I praised God for keeping me in perfect health. The symptoms left.

I thank God for the ministries that teach the truth about the gospel and about healing. People like me who have been raised in the traditional, mainline kind of church, have never heard that healing is a part of our salvation. I had never heard that God cares about me. I had always thought that God was mad at me.

It was those teachings that led me into a study of the scriptures where I learned the things I needed to know to live a victorious Christian life. Since I learned the truth in His word, He has done other wonderful, supernatural things in my life. Our family is doing wonderfully.

*   *   *

" Seek the Lord and His strength; seek His face evermore. Remember His marvelous works which He has done, His wonders, and the judgements of His mouth.."   Psalm 105:4-5

*" Hear my cry, O God; attend to my prayer. From the end
of the earth I will cry to You. When my heart is
overwhelmed lead me to the rock that is higher than I."*
Psalm 61:1-2

*   *   *

*" God is our refuge and strength, a very present help in
trouble. Therefore we will not fear, though the earth be
removed, and though the mountains be carried into the
midst of the sea; though its waters roar and be troubled,
though the mountains shake with its swelling, Selah."*
Psalm 46:1-3

*   *   *

*" Trust in the Lord with all your heart, and lean not on
your own understanding. In all your ways acknowledge
Him, and He shall direct your paths." Proverbs 3:5-6*

*   *   *

*" Open my eyes that I may see wonderous
things from Your law."   Psalm 119:18*

John Riggs

"Is anyone among you sick? Let him call for the elders of the church, and let them pray over him anointing him with oil in the name of the Lord. And the prayer of faith will save the sick, and the Lord will raise him up..." James 5:14-15

It was 9:45 a.m., Feb. 14, 1983 when I was shot. I was driving to work at the telephone company when I had a blowout on Northwest Highway and the Broadway Extension in Oklahoma City. I eased my car to the side of the road, and when I got it stopped I opened the door and was about halfway out when a van pulled up alongside of me. A man leaned out of the passenger side and shot me through the top of my head.

When that first bullet hit me everything went black. Then I heard another "POW " and I could feel blood running down my face. I knew what was happening to me. I had been saved for about two years, having given my life to Christ in January of 1981. My first thought when I realized I had been shot was that I was so glad I had given my life to Christ. "Here I come, Lord," I said. "Into Your hands I commend my spirit." I thought I was a dead man.

Immediately after I said that I came back into the light. There was a ringing sound in my head. I was laying face down on the shoulder of the road. I heard that "POW" again, and I felt the bullet enter the back of my head. I tried to get up, but I couldn't. I didn't know it at the time but I was paralyzed.

A construction worker from the other side of the road saw the whole thing, and he ran to help me. He turned my engine off, and he told me others were blocking traffic in that slow lane so I wouldn't be hit by a car as I lay there on the ground. He told me that the police and an ambulance had been called. He also told me that he had the license number of the van and a description of the men who shot me.

The Oklahoma City police were the first to arrive. I had slid part way under the car when I fell after that first bullet hit me, and they pulled me out. One of the officers asked me if I could hear him, and I told him that I could. They asked me if I knew what happened, and if I knew who shot me. I told them that I didn't know because I had not actually seen anyone.

As soon as they loaded me into the ambulance they began working on me. I heard the driver calling the hospital and telling them they were bringing in a shooting victim but that I would be DOA; dead on arrival.

While we were still on our way to the hospital one of the paramedics said to the other: "We are losing him." They put an oxygen mask on me, and started some other procedures. I don't know why it took me so long to get to it, but I finally started to pray.

As soon as they got me to the emergency room doctors and nurses gathered around to examine me. I asked the doctor if they had a chaplain, and to please bring him to me. I gave them my pastor's phone number and I asked them to call him. I also gave them my phone number at work and asked them to call and tell them what happened. Then I gave them the numbers of my mother and my fiance, even though I had three bullets in my brain. I was told later they were either .38 cal. or .45 cal., and that one was probably a hollowpoint judging by the way it fragmented when it went in my head.

Recently I had been listening to evangelists R.W. Shambach and to Kenneth Copeland on their tv programs as they taught on receiving physical healing and on how to pray the prayer of faith. I wanted someone to pray the prayer of faith over me. When the chaplain arrived I said to him: "Do you know what to do for me brother?" He said: "Yes, I'll pray for you." The Holy Spirit then showed me a scripture I didn't know in my natural mind. I had never read it or heard teaching on it, but I quoted James 5:14-15 to him: *"Is any sick among you? Let him call for the elders of the church; let them pray over him, anointing him with oil in the name of the Lord; and the prayer of faith shall save the sick, and the Lord shall raise him up; and if he has committed sins they shall be forgiven him."*

That was what I wanted; an elder of the church who would do what the Bible said, anoint me with oil and pray the prayer of faith over me. The chaplain told me he had no oil, but he would pray. My family was beginning to arrive then. The doctors were still examining me and taking x-rays. They didn't seem to know what to do. They were trying to decide. They had never seen anyone living with three bullets in the brain, and one of them fragmented. I was still alert and coherent even though they were giving me sedatives. I never did feel any real pain.

As they were wheeling me down the hall to surgery my

pastor, Willie Boone, arrived. He bent over me, and I asked him if he knew what to do for me. He said that he did. He anointed my head with oil, and he prayed the prayer of faith over me in the name of Jesus. It was 5:30 in the afternoon when they finally took me to surgery. They worked on me until after midnight.

While they were preparing me for surgery the anesthesiologist brought a paper over for me to sign giving him permission to administer the anesthetic. He told me there is always a chance you will not wake up from the anesthetic, and that my case was extremely serious with three bullets in my brain. All were in different areas, and one was shattered and fragmented into various places in the rear portion of my brain. They had x-rayed me and given me a CAT scan so they knew where the fragments were. The doctor told me the only thing I had going for me was that I was still conscious and he couldn't understand why.

I asked the anesthetist if he was going to put a mask over my face, and he said he would. I told him to please let me know before he put it on so that I could close my eyes and start to pray. I did not want to see him put that mask on my face. I told the doctor I would either wake up in the recovery room or I would wake up in heaven. He told me that he would be praying for me during the surgery.

I woke up in the intensive care recovery room about 8 a.m. I was only there for one day before they put me on a general floor. When I woke up my legs were paralyzed.

One day laying there in my hospital bed I was watching a tv evangelist teaching on forgiveness. I had been praying to be healed from the paralysis. I awoke about 2 a.m. with the spirit of the Lord moving on me to forgive the people who shot me. I tried to fool God. I told Him that I didn't want to do anything to them. I just wanted the police to catch them so they wouldn't hurt anyone else. Really I wanted to go out and find them and do something to them for what they had done to me.

When I tried to fool God the Holy Spirit came all over me in a way that I knew He meant business. "**I said forgive them,**" He told me. I started to cry then, and I sobbed out to the Lord: "Please help me because I can't forgive them." As I laid there in my hospital bed praying and crying I found myself saying: "Father, whoever they are, wherever they are, send someone to witness to them so they will be saved. I forgive them for what they did to me."

When I said that I felt something break loose inside of me. It was a release of calmness and peace that was so deep I cannot express it. I knew that God was going to heal me and that I would walk again. The next day a minister friend, The Rev. Herman Walker, came to visit me. Holding to his arm I took my first staggering steps in my hospital room. After receiving physical therapy treatments I was discharged from the hospital six weeks later with a walker which I needed for only a short time.

The night before I was discharged some friends and nurses and staff were in my room having a little party for me because I was such a miracle case and I was going home. A nurse from another floor came in, and when she saw me she just turned white and said: "I don't believe it." She had been on duty in the intensive care unit when they brought me back from surgery. She had been off duty when they moved me to the general floor, but she just knew I couldn't live. She had assumed I died when she was off shift, and when she saw me alive and well she just couldn't believe it.

I didn't know as much then as I know now about the word

of God and about how God works. I asked Him after I was out of the hospital why He had done all this to me. He quickly told me that He was not the one who did it.

I believe He is using this experience now to show me and others how great and almighty His power is if we will see and hear and believe. I promised the Lord that night that I would carry His word wherever I went, and I would go wherever He sent me.

Within six months of the shooting I was back on my job at Southwestern Bell Telephone Co. as a frame attendant. Shortly after that I was invited to preach my first sermon at Pleasant Ridge Baptist Church in Oklahoma City. Within nine months I was ordained. I continued for almost a year at my secular job when I was led by the Holy Spirit to enroll in Midwest Bible School. I was graduated from there in 1985. I was graduated in 1988 from Mid-America college with a bachelor of science degree, and have started my own outreach ministry: The Jesus Freedom Deliverance Ministry.

The men who shot me were never found. I still do not know why I was shot. The police have speculated it may have had something to do with a drug deal and a case of mistaken identity.

*   *   *

Leah Martin

*"Be doers of the word, and
not hearers only, deceiving yourselves,"
James 1:22*

When I was 13 months old my father was killed in an auto accident. My mother was seven months pregnant with my sister, I had pneumonia, and my grandmother was hemorrhaging with a bleeding ulcer. From those earliest days my mother instilled in me the idea that these afflictions were God's doing.

People say you cannot miss what you never had, but anyone who has done without a parent knows that is not true. You can very definitely miss having a parent you never knew. I missed my father tremendously. In that parental void I was drawn toward my heavenly Father at an early age. I would go out in the woods with my dog and sit for hours at a time having conversations with the Lord.

At ten years of age we were having a revival at our little country Methodist church. When the altar call was given no one responded. The Methodists have a way of going on with an altar call for what seems an eternity, especially if you are under conviction like I was.

As the preacher stood there pleading for someone to come

to the altar I thought I would help him out, so I went. My motives were not the purest, but the Lord knows what it takes to get us off our seat. My spirit was reborn. There was a definite change in my life from that time on. I had a zeal and enthusiasm for the Lord that drew me toward spiritual things. I realize now that can be a danger if you are not properly instructed because there are two spirits in this earth. There is the Holy Spirit, and there is an un-holy spirit. I had never been taught that the devil could speak directly to me, but he did.

My mother had a wild rose bush in the yard. Since I was athletic I decided I would jump over that bush every day all summer long. Wild rose bushes grow fast. I figured if the bush grew eight feet tall I would be jumping eight feet at the end of the summer. One day I was in midair over that rose bush, almost as if I were suspended there for a moment, and a voice spoke to me and said: "Someday you will have a tremendous physical handicap which you will have to overcome."

I reasoned it must have been the Lord who told me that. I didn't dwell on that piece of information. I went on through high school in excellent health and participated in many sports. I went into nurse's training. I did have some illnesses at that time which were attributed to "nerves." I was told an after effect of the illnesses was "bad nerves."

At the end of my training I met and married my husband and 18 months later our first child was born. Except for a very rapid labor of only one hour, and the fact she was three weeks early, all appeared to be normal.

Fifteen months after Tammy was born Kevin came into the world. He was two months early and weighed under five pounds. A few hours after birth he began having trouble breathing. It was thought at first to be his heart so we began to pray. On the second day I was told Kevin was somewhat better. I reached for the phone to call my mother and give her the good news, but as I put my hand on the phone a voice said to me: "Don't call her yet; you'll just have to call her right back."

I knew by that Kevin was not going to live. Again I thought it was the voice of the Lord. I went to the window and looked out, sun rays were streaming in and I really felt I was in the presence of the Lord. I said: "Lord, if You want Kevin, I am ready to give him up." In half an hour he was dead. At autopsy we learned Kevin had massive brain damage and would have been paralyzed from the neck down.

The doctors told us not to have any more babies for at least six months, but it seemed every time I went shopping I would see babies exactly the age Kevin would have been.

I prayed the Lord would strengthen my faith. I didn't know then that faith comes by hearing the word of God. We waited three months before I became pregnant. Again I went into premature labor at seven months, and ten months to the day that we buried Kevin, the same hour of the morning, the same day of the week, Brian was born. I was placed in the same bed in the same hospital room. He was in an isolette in the same spot in the nursery were Kevin had died. The same nurse was on duty.

Right after Brian was born the doctor came into my room, and I knew there was trouble. I said: "Lord, I cannot take it again." I prayed the problem would be in his lungs, and not be brain damage. The x-rays showed Brian had one collapsed lung and spots on the other. I figured the Lord was doing this to me to strengthen my faith. I didn't yet know that it is the devil who comes to kill, steal and destroy, and that it is God

who gives life and that abundantly. I didn't yet know that
God had given me authority over the works of satan.

Despite my ignorance I held onto one thought: Brian would
live. I constantly confessed he would live. On the third day
after delivery he was still hanging on but in critical condition.
I called our pastor for prayer, and at 9 pm the pediatrician
came into my room and told me the baby was just suddenly
breathing better. I looked at my watch and realized church
was just getting out. Prayers had been answered.

Three years later we wanted another baby, and with all the
problems I had we considered adoption. We completed the
paper work, and were waiting for a baby, but it began to play
on my mind; what if we would get a child and there would be
something wrong with it. I worried about that. I began to
pray in a different way: "Lord, let happen what is right." That
month — with contraception — our fourth baby was
conceived. Lisa was born five weeks premature and was just
an ounce over premature weight. After her birth I went back
to work in the hospital nursery even though I had a lot of
pain in my neck, shoulders, and back. X-rays revealed that
due to the type of labor I had the muscles, ligaments and
tendons from the back of my skull were torn. That was the
beginning of a multitude of problems. For the first time in
years I thought back to the time I was jumping the rose bush
and I heard that voice. I thought: "Well, here it is, that
tremendous physical handicap that God prepared me for."

I had several spinal discs out of place. I was told that if I
had any more children it would just rip my back apart. They
were urging me to have a surgical spinal fusion to alleviate
the problem. Then, at my insistence, I was given a more
thorough exam and it was discovered I had a retroflexed
uterus. The uterus was wedged against the sciatic nerve

causing my entire right leg, and my left leg to the knee, to be numb. I dragged the right leg as I walked. These problems went on over a year and I was being given Darvon, codeine, and Demerol among other drugs. A hysterectomy was done, and when I was discharged from the hospital, on the first morning home, I developed chest pains and a fever. I was readmitted to the hospital at my request, but the doctors did not believe I had a problem.

The nurse made rounds about midnight, and because she thought the room was stuffy, she opened my window wide. There was a defective call button, so I was not checked on again until six in the morning. It had rained during the night and it had turned cold and I had only a sheet over me. When they finally did check on me I was gray, spitting blood, and had a temperature of 103. My temperature went to 104 and over for ten days. I remember little of those ten days except for hallucinations. By x-ray they discovered I had a rather large blood clot in my lung which they believed caused the problem.

After I began feeling better I went back to work in the nursery, but I began to have weird symptoms. I would have thought I was pregnant except I had my uterus removed. The doctor told me that because I had just come through several serious medical problems I was tending to make too much of this.

One night in the nursery my legs just gave out from under me and I fell. This time I went to the doctor who was head of the obstetrical department, and he was the first person to really listen to me. He referred me to another doctor in the hospital whom I did not know and had never worked with. He wanted me to see a doctor who knew nothing of my medical history.

In August this man gave me a thorough physical. He ruled out brian tumor, lupus, and all of the obvious disorders. At one time he even told me that he could find nothing wrong. He told me to come right in the next time I had an attack, which I did. With a multitude of exams including dozens of blood tests he finally diagnosed multiple sclerosis.

He sent me to a neurologist in Columbus, Ohio, and he told them nothing about his diagnosis. He wanted a second opinion without implanting the idea of multiple sclerosis in the their minds. After one examination the neurologist confirmed the diagnosis. From that time on the attacks became more frequent.

In a very short time I was on crutches. The attacks were coming so often they began treating me with large doses of steroids to try to get me in remission. The steroid treatments were given intravenously with 2000cc of glucose. By the time the IV had been in about half an hour, if I were lying on my side, my head would be lopsided from the swelling. On a 1,000 calorie diet I gained about a pound a day under that treatment. At home I had to give myself steroid injections.

The effect of this was that I gained weight so rapidly I developed stretch marks over my body, some so large they looked like burn scars. My weight went over 200 pounds. Because my adrenal glands had quit working I couldn't lose weight. The doctors told me that if my adrenal glands were not functioning I could die of starvation and still be obese.

After a year I was put on a diet. I had been hospitalized again, and I had lost my vision. I could discern light, but I could not recognize anyone except by the sound of their voice. I was partially paralyzed. I had no small-muscle motion. I could not hold a telephone or a glass of water. I was on an 800 calorie diet with no salt, but I wasn't losing any weight because I was in bed all the time. For one six month period my caloric intake was reduced to between 300 and 500 calories. I lived on unsweetened pineapple, Cream of Wheat with artificial sweetener and powdered milk, an occasional piece of broiled hamburger or white meat chicken. On that diet I lost 70 pounds.

Due to my back condition it became very difficult to draw spinal fluid. One time at the Columbus hospital I counted 23 times the resident doctor attempted a spinal tap, and then I quit counting. There were several more attempts made before she completed the tap. Frequently I would have total body spasms. When that happened I would be taken back to the hospital for a Demerol or Valium injection. I was also taking a number of muscle relaxants. Once, when a new drug came out which they prescribed for me, I was taken off 23 other drugs. I had been taking 40mg of Valium daily for five years, and at times as much as 60mg a day. In order to cleanse my system, they took all those drugs away from me, cold turkey, and I went through a three day drug withdrawal period with my entire body in spasms. I braced myself against the bed with hands and feet and laid that way for three days. Later a doctor asked me if I remembered any of it because I had gone into a severe coronary reaction at the time. I remembered every second of it. It was pure hell.

During the course of the disease I had a terrible drug reaction. One of the drugs I was taking was allowing me to walk, but it was also keeping me awake since it acted on my nervous system. They were giving me sleeping pills so I could get some rest. Those pills, along with the Darvon and the others, including as many as six chloralhydrate a night, started a severe reaction.

I couldn't sleep. I had to be in constant motion. If I laid

down I had to bounce my arms on the bed. I couldn't keep my feet still. I would have to get up and pace. Weak as I was I couldn't do much of that. Sometimes when I laid down I had to thump my head up and down on the pillow. I went for one month with no sleep; literally no sleep at all.

Sometimes surges of energy would come up through my body from my feet and I couldn't control myself. Once when I was in the hospital in Columbus one of those surges hit me. There were windows from floor to ceiling. Under normal conditions I couldn't walk without crutches, but a surge hit me and I jumped from the bed and I wanted to go right through that window, but I grabbed the end of the bed and threw myself around the foot of the bed and out into hall and took off running down the corridor.

When that wore off they had to bring me back to my room in a wheelchair. I couldn't walk. That went on for months. I realized later it was satan trying to kill me. It seemed that every time I would receive some Bible teaching this type of thing would happen. Satan didn't want me to make any progress.

Then I was given experimental shock therapy in an attempt to stop the pain and prevent addiction to those pain-killer drugs. It was thought the shocks would help me to stand the pain, but really all it did was scramble my brain. To this day I have a year missing from my life. I don't remember leaving the hospital, or my birthday that year, or going home. The following year I was in the hospital in Columbus during my birthday, and when they asked me how old I was I gave my age as being one year younger. Later, at home, going over income tax papers, I argued with my husband about my age still thinking I was a year younger. I read books that I do not remember reading. I would pick up books and see where I had marked them all the way through, but I had no knowledge of what the book contained.

My doctor later admitted to me the shock therapy was a mistake; that it did more harm than good. We were spending hundreds of dollars a month on drugs and hundreds of dollars on dental bills because my teeth were all decaying at the gum line because of the drugs. I had severe headaches for weeks at a time. I cannot remember being without one, but sometimes it was just a little more bearable. I would sometimes lay for days at a time in a dark room with an icepack on my head. I couldn't tolerate light. I couldn't tolerate the slightest sound. To my ears any sound was noise. I spent one 18-month period flat on my back.

A friend asked me one day if I had ever heard Kenneth Copeland teach the Bible. I had no interest in it, but I didn't want to hurt her feelings so I turned on the program, and after that first time I listened every day. The first thing I learned from his teaching was that everything I needed in the way of healing had already been provided.

A preacher I knew would occasionally stop by to see me. Up to that time I had never told anyone about the voice I heard when I jumped the rose bush when I was a young girl. I told that preacher how God had told me that I was going to have a very serious physical affliction. He told me: "That wasn't the Lord. That isn't the way the Lord works." My mouth just dropped open. Later that preacher told me he didn't say any more at that time because I wasn't ready to receive it.

I was just totally shocked. I had not been actually taught that all inward voices are the Lord, but I believed it by implication. Later I heard another Bible teacher say these things are allowed in our life only insofar as *we* allow them.

That made me absolutely furious because that meant I was partly responsible for my condition. That wasn't the way I had been taught. I stopped listening to the teachers for a few days.

Then as I listened to Kenneth Copeland teach on healing and faith and the authority of the believer I began to see that satan had set me up. When I saw it I just stomped my foot. I yelled at satan, and I told him I was not going to stand for this physical harassment anymore. I began talking faith, and I guess I *talked* faith for two or three years before I acted.

It was on July 4th, 1980 that I stepped out in faith for my healing. I could do very little. Things were piling up. I said: "Lord, help me to get more work accomplished." In response to that simple prayer I heard a little voice inside me say: *"Well, get up and do it."* That wasn't what I expected to hear. I reasoned that couldn't have been the Lord. I couldn't see God speaking to an invalid person like that. I didn't like that message very well, so I let that word lay there for a couple of weeks. But, I could see so much that needed to be done for the family. Again, I just plopped myself down and said: "Oh, Lord, I have to get more work accomplished. Help me to get more done." He said: *"Well, get up and do it."* This time I knew it was God.

I answered Him: "Lord, how can I do it when I haven't the strength?" I had been listening to teaching on the laws of sowing and reaping, and through that teaching the Lord was saying to me sow strength and reap strength. I began to pray more earnestly, and to listen to the voice of God in my spirit. Under His direction I changed to a high fiber diet. I started an exercise program. That first day I did a few minutes of light warm up exercises, and then had to go back to bed totally exhausted.

I set my mind the next day to walk as far as I could without my crutches. I was able to walk across the street and back. I made a decision that I was going to go further each day than I had gone the day before, even if it was only one step. I took a rock and used it as a marker. I would walk as far as I could and put my rock down. The next day I would walk to where the rock was, pick it up and go a few steps further, and put it down again for the next day's goal. Two weeks after I started I put the crutches away. In six months I was going a mile. In nine months I was going two miles. Then I started running. I would run a mile and walk a mile. On really nice days I would ride my bike four miles.

I was on a lot of medication at that time, and I began to take myself off the drugs. Inderel, which is usually used for heart conditions, was prescribed for my severe migraine headaches. It had to be stopped gradually. I withdrew myself without my doctor's knowledge or consent. I was taking ten 65mg Darvon tablets a day for the pain, and began taking myself off of them. In the previous couple of years they had come out with a new drug for multiple sclerosis called Lioresol. It is amazing what that drug does for certain MS victims. Some people with MS never have pain. I had the spastic type, and without a muscle relaxant I would just curl up in a ball and it was extremely painful. I was in agony if I didn't have relaxants and pain medication.

Those ten Darvon were taking care of the overriding pain. I believe the Lord led me to withdraw from Darvon. I reduced the medication one pill at a time, but every time I reduced the daily intake I would go through three days of withdrawal. I began to wonder why, if the Lord was guiding me to do this, was I having withdrawal pains.

We were having a revival at the church I was attending, and

Larry Turner from Tennessee was preaching. He announced that at the end of the week he would hold a healing service. By Saturday I was running out of medication. I had one pill left. I was trying to decide whether or not to get that prescription refilled. My mind was telling me: "Tomorrow is Sunday, and you cannot get it refilled Sunday, and you know that if you go two hours without it you will be in agony. Tomorrow you are going to be a wreck. By Monday it will be pure hell. What if the healing service doesn't work for you?"

I decided I would not refill the prescription. I would go for my healing. Also, I had been taking laxatives for ten years. Another thing; I slept on what is called an Aquapad, which is a rubber pad about the size of a desk top with channels of heated water running through it. That helped me to sleep and soothed the painful muscle spasms.

Saturday night I was prayed for in the healing service. I heard others who had been prayed for tell of feeling the power of God go through them. I felt absolutely nothing. As I went back to my seat God clearly spoke to me and said: *"You have to get rid of that Aquapad."* Oh, how I wanted to keep that Aquapad. It was so comfortable to sleep on. We were renting it, and we returned it. When I went to bed that night I was aching all over.

I had made up my mind I was going for my healing. I started really claiming it. I started taking authority over the works of satan. I slept that night without the Aquapad. One month later, to the day, I had a real battle with pain. Right behind that satan came and told me: "See, if you had been healed you wouldn't be hurting like this. Why don't you just take a couple of aspirins. That wouldn't be like going back to your other medication."

I stood against that in the name of Jesus. I knew that I should not take as much as one aspirin. When that attack came I had my husband, our pastor, and an elder from the church lay hands on me and pray, and that was the end of it. The pain left. It was also amazing to come off the laxatives instantly after ten years, and with no side effects. When they prayed for me they bound the symptoms of withdrawal from appearing in my body, and I had no withdrawal symptoms. Then I realized I had symptoms of withdrawal when I came off the Darvon. It was because satan steals everything he can from you, and I didn't take authority over him. Every blessing you get from God satan will try to steal.

One of the turning points for me was when I saw in the book of James: *"Be ye doers of the word, and not hearers only, deceiving your own selves."* I had talked faith, and talked it; but what had I done about it? Faith without works is dead, the Bible says. The Bible also teaches that to he who knows to do something and then doesn't do it, to him that is sin. I had heard the scriptures over and over. I set my mind to believe the word of God is really true. Anything contrary to the word of God is a lie. Once you have light you are responsible to walk in it. I knew that I had received truth and if I did not walk in it my disobedience would become sin. It was that realization that finally blasted me out of my rut and got me walking in the spirit.

My healing was not instantaneous. I may never get a better report form my doctors than that I am in an excellent remission from multiple sclerosis. It is the nature of that disease to be into remission. However, I have been in remissions before when some of the symptoms would partially subside for a time, but in each of those cases when I tried to increase my level of physical activity I ended up flat on my back in the hospital in worse shape than I had been before. I had never been able to run or even walk for long distances.

As I write this I am working full time at an extended health care facility. I average two or three hours of overtime daily, and I am working on a college degree in business administration. I am going full steam, and I have no physical problems. In my last physical exam the doctors could find nothing wrong with me.

Last year I got new glasses for the first time in my life. Interestingly, they first diagnosed the MS through an eye exam when they discovered I had optic neuritis. There was a lesion on the optic nerve of my right eye. The ophthalmologist knew my medical history, so he gave me a very thorough exam. He told me that I do not have optic neuritis now. He also said that lesions of that kind do not normally just disappear. For me that exam was the final and total verification of my healing.

One of the ways satan works on us after we receive our healing is to bring back twinges of symptoms and inject thoughts into our minds. "It's that disease again. You are losing your eyesight again. Just like the first time. You are in for it now." When those thoughts came to me I learned to not voice them to anyone. I would reject them immediately. I overcame satan by the blood of the Lamb and by the word of my testimony, once I learned how, just as the Bible says.

When I went for that eye exam it was just to get a new eyeglass prescription because of the close paper work I was doing with my college studies and hospital record keeping. There was nothing wrong with my eyes except the normal aging process.

There is no known cure for multiple sclerosis. It is a

disease of the brain and spinal cord. Usually it is fatal. It is usually not rapidly fatal unless it is the fulminating type. With that kind the doctors normally give the patient from six months to a year to live.

When I had the disease my throat was partially paralyzed and I was weakened all over, but mostly on my right side. I had a bad case, and it was progressing rapidly by the time I got hold of the word of God. It doesn't really make any difference to me what the doctors call it. I know what it is.

One doctor with whom I discussed it told me it was just my will power overcoming the symptoms. It wasn't will power. It was God. I tried many times to help myself through will power, and it just didn't work. I give the Lord total credit for my healing.

It was Kenneth Copeland who first fed me the word of God and strengthened my spirit. I was so very weak, and my eyesight was gone, and I could not read the Bible for myself. Uttering a simple "yes" or "no" would totally exhaust me. There were times during that sickness — two or three days at a time — when I could do nothing but concentrate on taking my next breath.

I seriously considered suicide several times, but the Lord's hand was on me. I didn't know then what I know now. I know there is a spirit of suicide. After those feelings would leave me, I would look back and could not believe that I had actually been considering taking my own life.

During those times when that spirit was oppressing me I would count my pills and figure how I could take an overdose and make it look like an accident so my family wouldn't blame me. I would really work on plans like that when that spirit of suicide would harass me.

Those times when the symptoms tried to come back on my

body I kept my peace. I never told anyone. There were days when I had to force myself out of bed, and I think if I had not done that I would still be in bed. The symptoms were strong. I would grab hold of I Peter 2:24 and get up and do what I had to do.

Many people tried to tell me, after I was healed, that there never had been anything wrong with me. Even people close to me have told me to my face they believe I was never really sick. One woman even said the doctors had falsified my records. It seems so strange to me that people would rather believe a lie than believe that God can heal you.

*   *   *

"Forever, O Lord, Your word is settled in heaven. Your faithfulness endures to all generations..." Psalm 119:89-90

Barbara Wynalda

"...by His (Jesus') stripes we are healed..."Isaiah 53:5

When I was 17 — that wonderful teenage year — I was working on a suntan, and, like everything else you do at that age, I had to have it *right now*. I fell asleep under the sunlamp and burned my eyes very badly. It was just an act of stupidity. I was hospitalized for five days with my eyes swollen shut. The doctors thought I would never see again. There was a great deal of damage to the retinas.

Along with the physical damage to the eyes there was excruciating pain. I was put on strong pain-killer medication. My face was burned so badly that my eyes were almost a secondary consideration. My arms were also blistered. When they finally removed the bandages from my eyes I could see some, but things were blurry and I had to be fitted with prescription glasses. I was very thankful that I could see at all.

At the time I burned my face God was a part of my life, but I wasn't a Christian. My father told me once: "If you continue to talk about God in this house I am going to send you to a juvenile home." I would lay on my bed at night and cry out to God. I knew there was more to God than I was experiencing, but I didn't know how to reach Him. I would cry: "Help me, save me." I remember one time when it seemed that neither God nor anyone else was hearing me. I was a young frustrated teenager, and I said, in desperation: "Ok, devil, if you are there, you come in. Somebody talk to me."

That was a very dangerous thing to do, but I didn't know it then. God delivered me from that folly, but not until I was 23 years old, and by then I needed a complete deliverance. Since that time I have diligently searched the scriptures and I have grown.

Over the years, from the time my eyes were damaged, I would go periodically to have them examined. Always I was told the same thing; there is no change. The damage was still evident. But, neither did my glasses prescription change. The ophthalmologist told me that was strange because people's eyes become weaker as they get older, but mine were staying the same.

The doctor's didn't tell me very much at the time it happened. I was told that I had destroyed part of the retinas in each eye. My parents didn't ask the doctors many questions, and I never did get very many answers. I believe that was a blessing not knowing all of the factual medical reasons why I would never again be able to see clearly.

Following marriage, we attended two churches. We left the first because they weren't teaching the Bible. The second one we tried was absolutely dead. My husband had been brought up in an old mainline denomination. I knew there was more than I was getting in church. I craved a deeper spiritual life, but I didn't know what to do about it. I just couldn't get enough truth. One day we found the 700 Club on tv, and then we began to watch Lester Sumrall and Kenneth Copeland. Suddenly I was being fed. I had such a hunger. I still have that hunger. I was taking in a great deal of scriptural knowledge. I didn't know it at the time, but it was mostly going into my brain, and not my heart.

I had so much Bible knowledge that people began to come to me for counseling. I was able to pass information along to those who were seeking, and I was able to help them, but it didn't seem to be going very deep into me. I sent away for teaching tapes, and I would listen to them over and over again. Every time I listened the scriptures went a little deeper into me. There was a teaching on joy that especially helped me at that time. The Bible says the joy of the Lord is our strength.

Then, in April of 1986, I was almost 40-years old, the word of God suddenly became very real to me. Early that morning I was in the shower. I had finished my prayer time, Bible study and worship. I was listening to a tape of Kenneth Copeland's which I had listened to fifty times already. Suddenly I had a strong feeling deep down inside of me. It was saying: "Healing is yours. Take it now. Take hold of it. Hold onto it. Don't let it go."

There had been two or three times before when I had said aloud the fifth verse of the 53 chapter of the book of Isaiah: " But He was wounded for our transgressions, He was bruised for our iniquities; the chastisement of our peace was upon Him, and with His stripes we are healed."

This time, though, there was something different about it, and I couldn't let go. The following day I went for a drive in my car, and, of course, I was wearing glasses as I had since age 17. The Lord spoke to my spirit and said: "If you are healed you don't need glasses." I thought, oh, alright, I'll put my glasses in my purse, just in case I may need them later. As I slipped them into my purse the Lord said to me: "Don't you believe me?" At first I thought: "Oh, come on now." In my spirit I heard: "Do you believe me?" Then I answered that inner voice. I said: "Yes, I believe." I drove home and hid my glasses way in the back of a cupboard, and I haven't had them out since.

My eyes and my vision were healed then, but there were times over the next several months when I would be watching television, or sitting in church looking at the pulpit from a distance, and things would suddenly become blurry. I would get right on it in the spirit in prayer and say: "Satan, I do not receive blurred or imperfect vision. By Jesus' stripes I am healed." The blurring would always leave then.

One of the worst attacks came one night when I was driving home in a heavy rain, and I was having difficulty seeing the road. I stood on the word of God and simply prayed: "Lord, get me safely home." Of course the prayer was answered, and I was soon seeing perfectly again. Those attacks on my vision came at odd times for about four months, and I had to battle them in the spirit by the word of God.

It was difficult because we see with our eyes, and faith is believing without seeing. For that reason I think standing for healing of vision is one of the most difficult healings to stand for. It was difficult to maintain my faith because I had to see, and all the time satan was telling me: "You cannot see clearly so obviously you have not been healed. You don't have your healing. No, no, no." When I was standing for my healing all of my senses wanted to side with the devil and convince me I wasn't healed and probably never would be.

Gradually, as I fed my spirit on the word of God and on

teachings from several of the faith ministries, my faith began to grow. My faith for healing is now second nature. I am relaxed in it. I recently had a vision test for renewal of my drivers license. My vision is 20/20.

*   *   *

*" The Lord is near to all who call upon
Him, to all that call upon Him in truth. He
will fulfill the desire of those who fear Him:
He also will hear their cry, and will save
them." Psalm 145:18-19*

"Because you have made the Lord, who is my refuge, even the Most High, your habitation; no evil shall befall you, nor shall any plague come near your dwelling. For He shall give His angels charge over you to keep you in all your ways. They shall bear you up in their hands, lest you dash your foot against a stone."
Psalm 91:9-12

*   *   *

"For the Lord God is a sun and shield. The Lord will give grace and glory. No good thing will He withhold from them that walk uprightly." Psalm 84:11

*   *   *

"They cried unto the Lord in their trouble, and He delivered them out of their distresses." Psalm 107:6

*   *   *

"Give me understanding, and I shall live." Psalm 119:144

DEBBIE HALE

"...give attention to my words:
incline your ear to my sayings. Do
not let them depart from your eyes;
keep them in the midst of your
heart; for they are life to those who
find them, and health to all their
flesh." Proverbs 4:20-22

It was 1969 and I was a senior in high school when I first started having respiratory problems. I hadn't had any problems before that, but I just took real ill then. I was the drum majorette. Everything was looking good, and I just took sick. Now that I know about spiritual warfare I realize it was an attack of satan. There had been no prior symptoms; no reason for it. The doctors couldn't make a clear cut diagnosis. They said it was very strange because it didn't connect with my medical history. They just didn't know how to help me.

Finally they called the sickness "triad asthma." They compared it to walking pneumonia. They told me I must have carried it for a long time, and then the symptoms just erupted. I didn't know the word of God then like I do now, so I didn't have any idea how to get this affliction off me.

I was brought up in the Lutheran church and I always went

on Sunday. I knew Jesus was my Lord. I knew He was resurrected and had conquered sin. I knew He was born on Christmas. That was about it. I was limited; very limited. Because of the triad asthma I missed eight months of school in my senior year. I had a tutor who came to my bedside and helped me. They set up a telecommunications system between my home and the school. That had never been done before around here. Many people from the community helped me.

I could listen to what was going on in the classroom, and I could speak to the class and to the teacher. My tutor tested me to assure I was learning. I was bedfast like that for eight long months.

I prayed at that time. I tried to bargain with God. Many people in those kind of circumstances do that. I told God if He would just get me well I would work for Him. It was a time of desperation for me. I was so young, and the medical experts, the ones I looked to for the answer to my problems, told me they had no answers. I was just sent home to lie in bed. I remember a pastor from St Louis came to our home and gave me communion. I guess they thought I was dying. I just cried out then: "God, help me." I didn't know what to do.

After that I had many sessions with many doctors. I was being hospitalized 15 to 20 times a year. I had tanks of oxygen in my room, and I carried medications in my purse. I had 13 operations to keep the airways open so I could breathe. I was sent to Dallas, Texas for treatments, and then to The National Institute for Asthma Research in Denver for more advanced treatments. I was there for three months. Every system in my body started to break down. Organs had to be removed. I had treatments by laser, and they injected radioactive substances in my thyroid gland. They did abdominal surgery, and it seemed the surgeries just kept going on forever.

In 1973 I attended a Billy Graham crusade, and I made a fresh commitment, and I began to know the Lord in a more personal way. That was the turning point, but I still knew very little about spiritual things. I was a fighter, though, and I wouldn't give up. There were times when the angels came and ministered to me when I was bedridden. There were times when I would just crawl up into His lap and hold onto Him. That was how I got through the worst of it.

I would say to Him: "Lord, I just love You. I love You, Father. I praise Your name." I praised Him a lot, and despite my deteriorating health I was having some wonderful spiritual experiences.

It was when I was between 25 and 27 years old they were doing all the surgeries on me. I hadn't been well then for almost ten years, and I thought that was just the way I was going to have to live for the rest of my life. There was a whole list of physical afflictions they said I had. Some of them had to do with the asthma and some were due to side effects of drugs and medical treatments.

One of the things the doctors were very concerned about was osteoporosis. That is a condition where the bones just sort of dissolve. They lose calcium, and you are very prone to fracture. They said I had that very bad. There was pain connected with it when I tried to walk. If I bumped myself a bone could break or a blood vessel could rupture. That happened continually. It was just one attack after another to wear me down.

I was having a great deal of thyroid trouble. They told me it was overactive, and if they didn't do something to control it

I would die.   The sinusitis got so bad they drilled four holes in my skull to drain my sinuses and to hold down the infections so I could breathe. Next they told me my female organs were diseased and would have to be removed. They said I had endometriosis, so they surgically removed all of my reproductive organs. My eyes started to go next. I had developed cataracts, and everything was becoming dim. My body was just falling apart.

It was at that time that Kenneth Copeland came to St Louis to hold a three day teaching meeting. I was just beginning to learn what it meant to live by faith. I was learning how to stay continually on the Lord's lap.   I was becoming disciplined to offer praise continually to Him.   I was saturating my mind and my heart with the word of God. I was learning that you could pull down satanic strongholds with that word. I was beginning to see with clarity that my body had been riddled with disease by the attacks of the enemy. I was seeing my attitudes and my personality being changed by the word of God. I remember so well looking back to where I had been, and realizing I was really changing. I got excited because I knew then the word of God was really working in me. Hope was beginning to well up in my heart.

From that time on all you could see was the smoke from my heels as I ran toward God. I attended Kenneth Hagin's camp meeting in Tulsa, and that lifted me higher. I was working in the trauma unit of a hospital in Carbondale, Ill., but I couldn't keep up the pace. I wanted so much to help those who were being torn up physically as I had been. Even though I couldn't keep up a full work schedule then, I determined I was not going to quit. I stayed in the Bible, and I kept up the spiritual warfare against the things that were coming against me. I decided I would at least minister in my own household, if nothing else, and I knew the Lord would anoint that.

My actual healing was a long process. It wasn't overnight. I wished it were. It seems so nice to have the kind of miracle that is immediate. Parts of it were immediate. With my eyes it was immediate. When I knew they were healed I went straight to the doctor and had them tested, and the cataracts were gone.

I am still being healed progressively. It may continue until I shake off this flesh body that has been so badly attacked and go home to heaven. I was attacked before I knew the word of God. I had vital things taken from my body before I knew what the Bible said about it. When I left the hospital in Denver they had me on their surgery roster for two more operations. I said: "Lord, I cannot take anymore surgery. I am just not emotionally fit for any more. I am not going to have any more." They had wracked my body. They took everything I had to give.

At that time I picked up my Bible and vowed I would fight this thing with just the word of God. When I started, my faith was very weak. I started by reading 1 Peter 2:24 which says that Jesus bore our sin in His own body when they nailed Him to the cross, and that by His stripes — the beating He took — we were healed. I told God: "I don't know how this will work, Father, but Your word says that You cannot lie, and that's a promise and I take You at Your word. I take it as a child takes something from its dad. I just take it. I repent of the sin of unbelief. Like David, God, I am after Your heart. I need Your wisdom, like Solomon, and I going forward with You."

With the little knowledge I had I let go of the world's way

and chose God's way and began to put my weight on His word and build my faith in His desire and ability to heal me. From that time on healing progressed. I continued to minister to my family, and to teach them in the things I was learning.

I really thought at the time that might be the extent of my calling; just to my own family. I would be the spirit filled mother, and I would minister to my husband and children. Then, out of the blue, the hospital called and wanted me to come to work. I didn't think I could do it. I told them I couldn't work nights because I got too weary. They said that was ok, I could work days. I told them I couldn't work Sundays because that was my day of worship. They said I could have Saturday and Sunday off. They made every concession.

We live in a rural area of southern Illinois, and because I play piano and organ and am a praise and worship leader I get into all of the churches to participate in their services. I prefer the spirit-filled churches because I can praise more freely there. The other churches accept me because of my healing. That has opened many doors to me. They knew me when I was so ill. They were all on my side, rooting for me, sending me get-well cards and encouraging me.

Everyone knows me because this is a small community and I grew up here. Sometimes when I am telling people about Jesus they will say: "Yeah, Debbie, but you walk so close to the Lord because you were sick for such a long time." The accept me because they think my specialness is because I was sick and was healed by the word of God. I tell them that just isn't so. My specialness is because I have been born again, and they can be born again too. They can put the word of God in their hearts and mouths and it will work for them in their circumstances just as it has worked for me. It will work for anyone.   Anyone who will receive it can have it. When nothing else will work, the word of God will work.

It was 1969 when my body was first attacked. When you are going through those hard times you are just sure that you will never get over it. You feel sure you can never forget it. But the Lord has a beautiful way of erasing all that is horrible. That has happened to me. I can remember some of it, but it isn't real to me now. I am so blessed now. When I look back I cannot really believe it happened to me.   I went through it alright, but the viciousness of it is gone.

Now when something tries to come against me in life I just speak the word of God over the situation, and I let that word battle the circumstances. The Bible says there is power in the word, and there is. There are spiritual laws that work.

In my work situation I often quote scripture. People at work think there is so much wisdom in me, but it is the word of God in me. That's all it is. He has taught me that when I make a decision to make it based on what the Bible says.

In every battle over my body I let the word of God do the fighting. As far as I am concerned I am healed by Jesus' stripes. The word of God has settled that for me. It is settled for all eternity. Every day I thank Him that I am healed by Jesus' stripes, and I watch it happen.

Everyone can win. It is my desire to see everyone defeat satan and win. I love the Lord. I love that He has got me in this very special hospital where I work. I know of no other hospital that functions like this hospital. I have worked in secular hospitals, and this one is different. It is run by the nuns. They have a chapel, and if I go there to pray for a patient they approve because they have dedicated their lives to serving God too. I enjoy going to work. So many blessings occur here. I know it is God's favor, and not just some coincidence.

What is so terrible is that there are so many people who are sick. They don't know the Bible, and their flesh doesn't even want to hear about it. They are in the hospital, and do not have easy access to the scripture they need. That is a very lonely place to be.

I am so glad to be on the winning team. My heart is just humbled. I often wonder if there are others as saturated with God and as happy as I am.

*   *   *

*"Whoever has no rule over his own spirit
is like a city that is broken down and
without walls." Proverbs 25:28*

Lori Hanson

"For the word of God is living and
powerful, and sharper than any two
edged sword, piercing even to the
division of soul and spirit, and of
joints and marrow, and is a
discerner of the thoughts and intents
of the heart." Hebrews 4:12

In 1980 Lori Hanson began experiencing startling respiratory problems. She was developing pneumonia on a regular basis. She began coughing up blood. When she began coughing up bits of lung tissue, Lori became very frightened.

I went to many doctors. They all said the lung damage was from the numerous times I had pneumonia. But when it got so I was having real difficulty breathing I sought out a specialist, and he told me he suspected the problem was an hiatal hernia which was leaking stomach acids into my lungs. After conducting some tests, he told me that sure enough, it was an hiatal hernia.

The lung function tests also indicated I had a high degree of carbon dioxide in my lungs, and they were in such bad shape that they would never return to normal. The specialist also said they could try to repair the hole in my diaphragm, but they didn't hold out much hope for a permanent solution because such repairs frequently don't last. He also said I would have to be extremely careful about my environment. I couldn't tolerate air pollutants such as dust, smoke or smog.

I didn't like any of the things that doctor told me, so I went to another specialist; one I knew to be a man of God. He confirmed everything the first doctor said, and told me I should wear a respirator for the rest of my life. It would be a portable unit I would have to carry with me.

I had to quit my job immediately. I was working in a medical laboratory where there were a great many chemicals in the air . My husband and I were attending a church at the time that didn't believe in divine healing. I had even experienced healings in my life before, but nothing this major. Also, those healings were miraculous. I hadn't done anything to receive them.

A fear of dying had come over me. It seemed everything was pointing that way. At church we would be singing about the sweet by and by, and songs about going to heaven. I'd be sitting there in agony thinking about leaving my two children who were ages one and three at the time. The doctors told me I wasn't going to get any better, and that lung tissue wouldn't regenerate, and if you don't have any lungs you die. I'd just fall to pieces and have to go to the restroom and just sob.

I felt so alone then. Nobody would comfort me. The people from church were telling me to stay away from nutty teaching about healing. They would tell me about people they knew who had tried to get healing through spiritual methods and how they died anyway. But at that time I came into possession of some tapes that explained healing. I just thank God that I got those tapes before I got too much indoctrination from our friends at church

Some strangers gave me a set of Gloria Copeland's tapes on healing and she was teaching how to use the word of God to attain your healing. I'd never done that. It was new information to me. I didn't really think it would work. I'd had so much religion pumped into me that just didn't make any sense to me. I reasoned that if God wanted me healed that He would just heal me. Because I wasn't healed, I assumed I was to suffer for His glory.

I also reasoned that I had nothing to lose by following this strange new teaching of hearing what God had to say in the Bible about my healing, and doing what He said. I learned that we are to take His word and hide it in our heart, we are to say it with our mouth, and build our faith in that way.

I learned some of the scriptures on healing, and I began speaking them aloud to myself: "By Jesus stripes, I was healed, He bore my iniquities, and my sin, and I don't have to bear them." I searched the scriptures for everything God had to say about healing. He said that He would withhold no good thing from those who walk uprightly before Him. I clung to that.

I was in extreme pain. My chest felt like it was burning. I would try to ignore it as I spoke the word of God concerning my condition. I would say to myself: "Lori, you are being healed. This is not the way you are going to be for the rest of your life. The word of God is true, and you are being set free." I talked myself into believing the word of God. Then, one day all of the symptoms were gone. The pain was gone. I could breath without the machine. I felt good. I called the doctor and told him my symptoms were gone, and I wasn't going to need surgery. That was two years ago, and I haven't been back to see him.

It took three months from the time I received the teaching on healing until my healing was manifested. One thing I learned was that the Bible says if we resist the devil he will flee. What struck me was that I had to resist him. I had to resist his works. I had to resist what he was doing to me. I resisted him, and praise God, my lungs are healed. I've maintained my healing by continuing to stand on the word. On several occasions symptoms have tried to come back, but I just keep saying, and believing, that by Jesus' stripes I am healed. I am learning more and more how to keep sickness from my family and how to maintain my healing. I see it working with my children as I teach them.

*   *   *

*"The Lord takes pleasure in them that
fear Him, in those that hope in His mercy."
Psalm 147:11*

Nancy Whitsitt

"Praise the Lord, call upon His
name declare His deeds among the
people, make mention that His name
is exalted. Sing to the Lord, for He
has done excellent things; this is
known in all the earth."
Isaiah 12:4-5

It was 5:45 Wednesday afternoon, March 26, 1986, and
my husband, Tim, had just gotten home from his job as
business administrator for an office supply firm in Tulsa,
Oklahoma. Tim played with Benjamin, our 16-month-old
toddler, for a few moments, and then he came into the
kitchen with me. Our other son, Landon, was at a
neighbor's, and the two girls, Allison and Betsy, had just
come in from play.

It was a few minutes before six o'clock when we missed
Benjamin. We looked through the house for him, but
couldn't find him. I wondered if he could possibly have
gotten outside. I went to the rear door, which is in a small
laundry room, and I saw it was ajar. Usually it is closed and
latched so he couldn't get out.

It seemed like I was out on the rear deck in one step, and I

immediately saw Benjamin floating face down in the hot tub.
I had turned the heat up in the tub about half an hour earlier
because we were going to use it that evening. I screamed as I
rushed to the tub and pulled him from the water. I kept
screaming, as if that would bring an end to the nightmare. In
a moment Tim was by my side and I handed Benjamin to
him. I had already noticed that he was not breathing.

He leaned the baby back to see if he would gasp or breathe
like you would coming out of the water after holding your
breath, but he didn't breath. His eyes were open and rolled
back in his head. While Tim held the baby I went straight to
the telephone to call for help. We had a long extension cord,
and as I called for the paramedics I stood by the back door
and watched Tim feel for a heart beat. There was no
heartbeat. Tim put his ear to Benjamin's chest to hear if he
was breathing, but he wasn't breathing. Tim prayed a very
simple prayer then: "God, give me strength, and give me
wisdom."

Immediately after he prayed Tim began to give the baby
cardiopulmonary resuscitation. We found out later that the
way Tim performed CPR was exactly the way you are
supposed to do it on a baby. It is different for an adult. With
a baby you cover both the nose and mouth with your mouth
when you breath into them. The Lord was leading Tim.
When he prayed for wisdom he got it. Tim had also pushed
on the baby's tummy to expel the water he had swallowed,
and we found out later that was also the right thing to do.

While I was on the phone with the paramedics Benjamin
began breathing in a very shallow way. It seemed like an
eternity before he began the shallow breathing. We figured
later he could have been in the water for over fifteen minutes.
We don't know for sure. It took the paramedics twelve

minutes to get to our house, and, though Benjamin was then breathing shallowly, he was still unconscious.

The paramedics had a portable oxygen apparatus that they hooked him up to, and they also used a stomach pump to get more of the water out of him. Because we lived way out in the country south of Tulsa, they called for a life-flight helicopter to take Benjamin to the hospital. We had to wait for that, and again it seemed like an eternity, but we knew it would be faster than trying to take him by ambulance through city traffic.

Tim flew with Benjamin in the helicopter, and the moment they landed at St Francis Hospital a medical team met them and rushed him to the emergency room. When I arrived later by car Benjamin was crying, but his eyes were glassy. His pupils were fixed, and he wasn't seeing anything. His limbs were stiff. I was told later these were further evidence of severe brain damage caused by lack of oxygen. The doctors had him hooked up to all kinds of tubes. They were giving him IVs and oxygen, and they pumped his stomach again. At the time it looked to me as if he had eighteen zillion tubes in him.

Dr. George Moore, at that time chairman of the Department of Medicine at the City of Faith Hospital in Tulsa, and a friend from our church, met us at the hospital and helped us through those first rough hours. He is a very good doctor, and he was a great comfort. He didn't tell us anything of the seriousness of Benjamin's condition at that time. After it was all over he told us that he was sure Benjamin had suffered severe brain damage from oxygen starvation. He exhibited all the symptoms of brain damage. Later the doctor from the emergency room told us the same thing.

The idea of Benjamin having brain damage hit me like a ton

of bricks. When I first discovered the medical staff believed he was brain damaged I wrestled with that concept in my mind for about two hours. As I prayed about it the Lord showed me that He wasn't going to give Benjamin's life back and not make him one hundred percent whole. Then I settled it with God, and I knew that everything was going to be all right.

I said to the Lord in that prayer that all I wanted right now was for Benjamin to wake up, recognize me, and say "Hi." That was the only word he knew. At 6 a.m. the morning after the accident Benjamin was in the intensive care unit, and the nurses were taking his vital signs just before the shift change. I watched as they tried to wake him. His limbs were still rigid, and all the other signs of brain damage were also still apparent.

As the nurses were tending him he stirred, opened his eyes, rolled his head toward me, and said "Hi." He then tried to climb out of the crib. At 16 months that was his entire vocabulary. It was the most wonderful word I had ever heard in my whole life. Not only was he saying something out of his memory, he showed that his brain was working in order to recognize me and put it all together. We began to rejoice, and we could see the stiffness leave his arms and legs. The nurses were astonished.

I had to leave the hospital shortly after that and collect our other three children from the neighbors and get them off to school. Tim stayed with Benjamin while a doctor gave him a thorough exam there in the ICU. The doctor told Tim that he was astounded, and that he could hardly believe the sudden and unexpected recovery.

Tim asked the doctor to explain that statement, and he told Tim that when he had examined the baby in the emergency room the night before he was sure he had major brain damage. The doctor also told Tim that it was a good thing he knew CPR because that was what saved the baby's life. Tim told the doctor he didn't know CPR. The doctor then said: "Well, you knew something." Tim told the doctor he had received wisdom and guidance from God that showed him what to do to save Benjamin's life.

About noon the nurses moved Benjamin into a regular hospital room. They watched him closely for the rest of the day, and the next morning he was released. The doctors said there was no reason to keep him in the hospital any longer. They sent him home a day and half after the accident and he hasn't had a problem since.

We did a lot of praying during that time. Many others were also praying for Benjamin. There are many sidelights to this testimony. One of them is that prior to the accident we had become involved in a teaching ministry on praise and the power of praise in our daily lives. We had been practicing that. Half an hour before the accident I was standing at the kitchen sink preparing supper and praising the Lord. The kids were wandering through, and they were praising the Lord with me. Then the accident happened.

It was comforting to know that when something like this does happen in your life that your position and relationship with God is such that you don't have to get on your knees and bargain for your baby's life.

I screamed when I saw Benjamin floating face down, and it was as if my heavenly Father came running to my aid. It was like Benjamin's daddy running to help. That's the way I felt it.

While Tim was performing CPR on the baby I was on the phone with the paramedics. They would put me on hold, and then come back on the line to check on things, and then put me on hold again. During those times I was on hold I prayed in the spirit for the Lord to give Tim wisdom and guidance so he would know what to do to help Benjamin.

When the ambulance was on the way with the paramedics was when they wanted me to hang up the phone. I told them that if something happened I wanted to have them on the line so I wouldn't have to waste time re-dialing. They put me on hold when they had to, and then checked back with me every few minutes. While I was on hold I prayed.

When the accident happened my girls were in the house. Knowing that I would not have patience to answer questions from five and six year olds at a time like that I told them to go to their rooms, but they had heard me praying, and they were curious.

At one point I had said: "God, you've given Benjamin to me; why are you taking him from me?" Immediately He said to me: "I am not the one trying to take him." Instantly I understood, and I knew what the situation was. I commanded: "Satan, you cannot have my baby. Take your hands off my baby."

When my girls heard me say that they wanted to know what was going on. When things calmed down to the point where I could explain it to them I simply told them Benjamin had fallen into the hot tub, and because he couldn't swim he was pretty sick and needed prayer.

My youngest daughter, Betsy, who was five, said to me that she wanted to know about the fire. I told her there was no fire. She said: "I saw a fire." I told her again there was no fire. She pointed to the laundry room, which was where the door is leading to the deck and the hot tub. She insisted she had seen a fire there in the laundry room. That was when I had been standing there talking on the phone to the paramedics and praying in tongues.

I didn't think too much about that incident until it was all over and I was telling it to a friend. She asked me if I had been praying when Betsy saw the fire. I told her I prayed every time they put me on hold. She told me that what Betsy saw was the spirit of the Lord in the form of fire. Of the three kids, the one who saw the ball of fire was the most calm during the whole thing. She was not upset in the least.

That night the children were staying at a friend's house, and Betsy wanted to go to bed even before bed time. The other two were distressed and cried a lot. I believe that Betsy was calm because she saw the Lord. She may not have known that was what she saw, but the vision had given her assurance and peace. The next morning when I picked them up for school the first thing Betsy said to me was: "Mommy, Benjamin is going to be ok." She said it with assurance as if she had inside knowledge. It wasn't a question. It was a statement of fact.

One thing I remember vividly was a teaching we had been listening to on revelation knowledge. It was by Kenneth Copeland, and he said that when God makes a promise, it is done. All you have to do is receive it and thank Him for it. You don't have to bargain with Him about it like so many try to do: "Lord, if You do this for me, then I will do that for You." Because of those teachings I felt the Lord had given us promises for which all we had to do was stand in faith and receive.

There was a financial miracle connected to the incident. We didn't have any insurance, and we had some pretty hefty hospital bills. We are tithers. We had learned not only to pay tithes, but *how* to pay tithes. We had learned not to be mechanical about it, but to worship God with our tithe, to take communion over it, and to handle it as a holy thing. We had just begun doing those things, and we were seeing our financial situation turn around in a number of small ways. Then came the accident and the large medical bills with no health insurance to cover them.

A woman heard about our situation and paid the entire bill. I really feel the Lord was honoring the things we had been learning and putting into practice.

I don't ever want to go through anything like that again, and it may sound strange, but I'm glad I did go through it once. It was an exciting spiritual experience to be put into a position where you absolutely have to trust God. It has made my faith rock solid. The power of God's word isn't just some theory I read about in a book. I have experienced it.

＊   ＊   ＊

"You will show me the path of life. In Your presence is fulness of joy. At Your right hand are pleasures for evermore."
Psalm 16:11

John Scott

*"So then faith comes by hearing,
and hearing by the word of God."*
Romans 10:17

Being raised in an Assembly of God church, and brought up by Spirit filled parents who love God and one another with all their hearts really gives a boy a head start, and I should have a testimony of how I served God all of my life, but I don't.

At age nine I received Christ as my savior, and was steady for about four or five years. As I entered my teens the devil made a play for me, and being spiritually ignorant and not recognizing the trap, I fell for his deceitfulness and served him faithfully for 20 years.

I began to hunger for knowledge. I began a long journey through one far eastern religion after another. I delved into Rosecrucianism and then into I Ching. I began to smoke and drink and life became wine, women and song, but I knew I was missing it somehow.

There was this nagging thought forever in my consciousness: "What would dad and mom think about me doing this?" That thought kept me from doing worse things than I did.

All through my different phases of truth-seeking I would try to convert my mom and dad, but she would just say: "Son, you know God said that if I would train up my child in the way he should go that he will not depart from it when he is old."

I thought she was some kind of nut. Yet, she never got angry or upset with me. She would just repeat that scripture to me and tell me that she believed God.

About 1970 I became interested in astrology, and I threw myself into the study of it with my whole being. I thought this is *IT*. I have found the truth. I know how to tell how everything happens and what will come to pass in the future. I have it made. I began plotting charts for all my friends and for all of my clients. I graduated from college in 1971 as a CPA and we moved to Jacksonville, Florida. Several of my clients were on the New York Stock Exchange.

I began advising by the stars all who came to me, and over a period of a few short years It got so about everything I said came to pass. I believed that because everything I was saying was coming to pass that I had the truth. I didn't understand at that time what God had to say about this in the book of James and the book of Mark. I learned that later.

I married in 1971 when I was a senior in college, and I really believe my wife was sent by God. Teddy was forever tugging at my sleeve telling me that astrology was of the devil, and that I shouldn't be messing with it. Of course I didn't listen to her. I told her God wanted me to know all there is to know, and since He gave me this thirst for knowledge it must be His will that I learn all these things.

In all of the astrology instruction I received I was taught mainly the negative aspect of charting. The teachers said anyone can handle good news, that is never a problem, so don't even bother with that. Dwell on the bad news so that people can watch out for it and prepare for it. To my ear that explanation sounded right at the time. I became very proficient at proclaiming bad news. I didn't understand then that *"faith cometh by hearing and hearing by the word of God,"* Romans 10:17. I also didn't know that fear cometh by hearing the words of the devil.

I went everywhere telling bad news and thinking I was helping mankind because the things I was saying were coming to pass. Our first daughter, Laura, was born March 3, 1972, and shortly after that I did a chart of my wife and informed her that after our second child was born — which would be a girl — my wife would come down with an incurable blood disease.

Teddy once asked me if I ever saw anything good in anyone's chart. I told her yes I did, but I had been taught that anyone can handle good news. It is the bad they have to prepare for. Then she told me that one of the women I had previously charted and her sister were coming over to be charted again. She said they were both on the verge of despair. Their marriages were on the rocks. One's child was hospitalized with a severe malady which I told her would happen. God forgive me. It doesn't take much to make a believer out of someone when signs follow the words you speak. You simply tell a person thus-and-so is going to happen, and when it does that person is hooked.

My wife told me these women had enough problems, and she made me promise to withhold the bad news and tell them only the good. I promised, but it was one of the most difficult things I ever did. If it had not been for Teddy sitting there with her eyes fastened on me as I did those charts, I don't think I could have kept that promise.

I did keep my promise, and I told both ladies only the good things pertaining to them and their families. As time passed only the those good things came to pass. All of the bad that I saw in their charts, but didn't tell them about, didn't happen.

I didn't understand that. The good happened, but the bad did not materialize, even though I had seen it in the chart. I was one confused astrologer.

I was taught that accuracy is imperative in charting the degree of the ascendent or rising sign. It is said to be one of the keys to understanding personality. But, as I began to experiment I would prepare a chart on a person and only tell them the bad I saw and not reveal the good. In those cases only the bad came to pass. With the next person I would prepare chart, forget the bad, and only tell them the good. Sure enough, the good would come to pass, but not the bad.

I concluded that accuracy didn't matter much. I stopped doing charts and simply began doing cold readings out of the Ephemeris which is a book of charts that discloses where every planet and the sun and moon are positioned at noon Greenwich time for a five year period. With that method I didn't go through the mechanics of laying out a chart.

By that time I had prepared so many charts that I could still see them in my mind's eye. I had just given up the accuracy of computing to the exact degree all of the planet and house positions. This phenomenon persisted in holding true in my dealings with people, and I became very reluctant to tell anyone anything bad. I got to the point where I was only telling good news because I thought I had come into possession of a special power, in and of myself.

I also began to think that if I said something it would come to pass. Little did I know that I was stumbling onto a universal truth of God found in Mark 11:23. So I began to watch my words. I even refused to think about anything I did not want to see materialize in the physical world.

Early in 1976 my dear wife, Teddy, who is a registered nurse, had a blood test as a favor to a lab technician who needed to practice. Later in the day the technician and the emergency room physician came to Teddy and told her not to leave the hospital because there was something wrong with her blood.

I began to understand what Romans 10:17 means in saying that faith comes by hearing God's word. The word my wife received was not God's word, but the devil's word. Faith didn't come. Fear came. When Teddy called I told her not to worry about anything. I told her everything was going to be alright. I told her that the hospital she was in was like MASH, so come on home and help me with these babies. Laura was three then and Katherine was two.

Everyday Teddy had more blood work done, and with every test the prognosis grew more grave. She finally was tested by a blood cancer specialist. He said the condition was very serious; that he would have to hit it with everything at his disposal. He ordered bone marrow tests.

Following those tests she was told she had about six months to live. That was the greatest shock we ever had to face. All Teddy could do for several days was sit and look at our two precious babies and wonder how I was going to be able to take care of them and give them the mother-love children so desperately need after she was dead.

I told her: "Honey, everything is going to be alright. I'll do whatever it takes to get you healed. I'll go wherever we have to go. Somehow, someway, everything is going to be alright."

We heard about the great staff at Ochsner Clinic in New

Orleans so we went there for a week of tests. After all the testing we had our exit conference with the head of the hematology department. He had already informed us that the doctor in Pensacola who had originally diagnosed the disease had completed his residency under him and that he was a very capable doctor. During this conference he let us know that he had nothing to add or delete from the initial diagnosis. Teddy was going to die soon. End of case.

After many days of sorrow and anger and all of the other emotions associated with this type of news I had to get back to work. Driving to the office I turned on my car radio and got WHYM, a Christian station, and it seemed as if God Himself was speaking to me. Kenneth Copeland was telling about the power of the tongue, and he said: "YOU HAVE WHAT YOU SAY." It went off inside me like a stick of dynamite. That is Mark 11:23 *"...I say to you, whoever says to this mountain, 'Be removed and be cast into the sea,' and does not doubt in his heart, but believes that those things he says will come to pass, he will have whatever he says."*

My entire life passed before me in a flash as vividly as if it were happening all over again. I saw as far back as I could remember where I had spoken words that had come to pass. Event after event passed before my eyes in rapid succession. The revelation knowledge of the source of the awesome power behind all things was made real to me. The final part of that vision was where I had done the astrological chart on my wife four years before and then told her she would come down with an incurable blood disease after our second child was born. The final words I heard during that vision that morning were: "And, you have what you say."

I was made aware that I was responsible for the disease coming on my wife. I didn't fully understand the way everything worked, but I did know that I had what I said. The next moment I was screaming at the top of my lungs, with tears flowing down my face: "Father, I don't know all of the sins I have committed, but I confess them all to you." I began to empty my heart to God. I came back to God at that moment yelling at the top of my lungs: "I have what I say, and I say my wife is going to live and not die."

I couldn't get back home fast enough. I ran into the house and grabbed Teddy by the shoulders and looked her straight in the eye and said: "Honey, you are going to live and not die." She looked me right back in the eye and said: "Oh, thank God, thank God." She began to weep with a complete release. We went to the medicine cabinet and pitched all the blood medication into the trash.

Teddy went to the Wednesday night service of the church in which I was raised. The pastor had the entire congregation stand before the alter at the beginning of the service and while beautiful organ music filled the sanctuary he began to quote from the 103rd Psalm: *"Bless the Lord, O my soul; and all that is within me, bless His holy name. Bless the Lord, O my soul, and forget not all His benefits: who, forgiveth all thine iniquities; who healeth all thy diseases..."* Teddy heard those words as though God Almighty had just uttered them to her personally. The pastor and the members of the church laid hands on her and prayed and God healed her there in Brentwood Assembly of God Church in Pensacola.

A few days later I called Kenneth Copeland's office in Fort Worth, Texas and ordered all of his teaching tapes. I devoured them. Some I listened to twenty times or more. A series called "The Power of the Tongue" I listened to until I almost had it memorized. Faith came. It kept coming and coming, because faith comes by hearing the word of God.

The manifestation of Teddy's healing was not instantaneous. We didn't see any changes for the better in her physical body for some time, although we continued to stand on the fact of her healing from the moment she was prayed for at church. The doctors had said the disease would progress over a period of time, and the final stage would be uncontrollable bleeding for which they could do nothing.

The symptoms progressed just as the doctors said. Teddy and I continued to stand in agreement that she was healed; not going to be healed, but already healed. We just couldn't see the manifestation of it yet. On October 30, 1976, six months to the day from when the doctor told her that he could not guarantee her six months of life, she began to hemorrhage profusely and uncontrollably.

I was out of town at the time. She called me and described what was happening. I said: "Honey, I don't know what is causing the bleeding, but you are healed. You do not have a blood disease." I told her to go to her gynecologist, but to not go to the hematologist who had given her the bad report.

When she went to the gynecologist he told her that he knew of her diagnosis. He told her to get back to the blood doctor. He said he didn't want the responsibility. Teddy told him she didn't know what was causing the hemorrhaging, but it wasn't the blood disease because she was healed from that.

The doctor agreed then to examine her and in doing so he ordered a complete blood work up. His examination revealed the hemorrhaging was caused by an ovarian cyst that had ruptured and was draining and needed no further attention. The blood tests revealed she was totally and completely normal. No trace of a blood disease. Exactly six months had passed.

Old slewfoot really tried, but, praise God, the word of

God works. The thing I was shown by God through the Bible and this experience is how astrology works. I have talked to several groups of astrologers since I learned astrology is an abomination to God. I told them it is an abomination to God, and it is an abomination to me.

Luke 5:15 says: *"But so much the more went there a fame abroad of Him, and great multitudes came together to hear, and to be healed by Him of their infirmities."* Jesus went about doing good and a fame spread of Him throughout the land so that those who heard came believing they would be healed and they were, and Jesus said to several: *"Thy faith hast made thee whole."*

In the world of astrology a fame went out about me, and people heard that whatever I said came to pass. Therefore they came believing based on hearing from others, and they then heard the words I spoke to them. They believed those words and went away telling others what was going to come to pass in their lives.

Mark 11:23 says that if you speak words, believing in your heart, what you say will come to pass, then you will have whatever you say. So these poor innocent people were coming to me, and I was deceived because I believed that what I said was true. I was telling them words. They believed my words, and made them their own words, and spoke the very things I said into existence in their own lives; good or bad. James 3:6 tells us that we set the very course of nature by our tongues.

God has shown me that is how all the philosophies of the world work. However, Jesus said that we should take heed what we hear because He knew that if we hear something without being firmly convinced of who we are and what we believe we may be deceived into believing a lie just as I was.

"*Whatever things were written before were written for our learning, that we through the patience and comfort of the scriptures might have hope.*" Romans 15:4

*   *   *

"*Seek the Lord while He may be found, call upon Him while He is near,*" Isaiah 55:6

If you have a testimony

which you feel

will encourage, strengthen

and edifiy others

please send it to

Stepping Stone Press
164 S. Highland Ave.
Pearl River, N. Y. 10965

"For I know the thoughts that I think toward you, says the Lord, thoughts of peace and not of evil, to give you a future and a hope. Then you will call upon Me and go and pray to Me and find Me, when you search for Me with all your heart." Jeremiah 29: 11-13

NOTES

NOTES

NOTES